Polymer Clay
EXTRAVAGANZA

LISA PAVELKA

NORTH LIGHT BOOKS
CINCINNATI, OHIO
www.artistsnetwork.com

about the author

isa Pavelka is a self-taught, award-winning artist, and her work is collected throughout the world. After leaving her career as a television producer and director after the birth of her second child, Lisa became serious about her artwork during her extended maternity leave. Friends soon began to commission her work. Success inspired her to start her first company, Bearly There, where she produced a line of hand-sculpted polymer clay figurines that sold in stores throughout the country. After nine years of working as a production artist, she began working as a polymer clay designer. Lisa designs craft kits and artwork for advertising, writes for several national magazines and makes frequent television appearances. Specializing in commissioned work, she also sells through galleries and was recently asked to contribute one of her pieces to the White House. Lisa is the founder and president of the Las Vegas Polymer Clay Guild. When she is not working in her studio, Lisa devotes her time to teaching art to underprivileged children through the House of Blues Foundation and other charitable organizations.

Polymer Clay Extravaganza. © 2002 by Lisa Pavelka. Manufactured in China. All rights reserved. No part of this book may be reproduced in any form or by any electronic or mechanical means including information storage and retrieval systems without permission in writing from the publisher, except by a reviewer, who may quote brief passages in a review. Published by North Light Books, an imprint of F&W Publications, Inc., 4700 East Galbraith Road, Cincinnati, Ohio 45236. (800) 289-0963. First edition.

Other fine North Light Books are available from your local bookstore or art supply store or direct from the publisher.

06 05 04 03 02   5 4 3 2 1

Library of Congress Cataloging-in-Publication Data

Pavelka, Lisa
    Polymer clay extravaganza / Lisa Pavelka
        p.cm.
    ISBN 1-58180-188-2
    1. Polymer clay craft. I. Title.

    TT297 .P33 2003
    731.4'2--dc21
                                    2002075189

Editor: Catherine Cochran
Designer: Stephanie Strang
Production Coordinator: Sara Dumford
Production Artist: Donna Cozatchy
Photographers: Al Parrish and Christine Polomsky
Photo Stylist: Jan Nickum

metric conversion chart

TO CONVERT	TO	MULTIPLY BY
Inches	Centimeters	2.54
Centimeters	Inches	0.4
Feet	Centimeters	30.5
Centimeters	Feet	0.03
Yards	Meters	0.9
Meters	Yards	1.1
Sq. Inches	Sq. Centimeters	6.45
Sq. Centimeters	Sq. Inches	0.16
Sq. Feet	Sq. Meters	0.09
Sq. Meters	Sq. Feet	10.8
Sq. Yards	Sq. Meters	0.8
Sq. Meters	Sq. Yards	1.2
Pounds	Kilograms	0.45
Kilograms	Pounds	2.2
Ounces	Grams	28.4
Grams	Ounces	0.04

I DEDICATE THIS BOOK TO MY HUSBAND AND BEST FRIEND, ALLEN, WHO MAKES ALL THINGS POSSIBLE FOR ME; TO MY MOTHER, KAROLINE FREED BIGGS, FOR HER NAIL FILE AND FOR ALWAYS BELIEVING IN ME; AND TO MY CHILDREN, JEREMY, NICHOLAS, DANIELLE AND ANNE, WHO MAKE ALL THINGS MATTER.

acknowledgments

Undertaking the writing of a book was a dream come true. The road that led to my career as an artist has been full of serendipitous events and unexpected surprises. I would like to take the opportunity to thank those people who have made such a large impact in my life.

Thanks from the bottom of my heart to my amazingly talented brother, David Freed, who always saw the artist in me. I'd also like to express my appreciation to my hubby for all of his help, and to my stepfather, Howard Hilt, for his unfailing support.

My eternal thanks to the folks at Polyform for providing all the clay used in this book: the late Chuck Steinmann, Wayne Marsh, Jan Walcott and Hope Phillips.

I'm immensely grateful to my dear friends in the polymer clay world who have encouraged and inspired my growth as an artist: Bev Sims, Maria Del Pinto, Audrey and Jimm Freedman, Kim Richards, Donna Kato, Gwen Gibson, Barbara McGuire, Katherine Dewey, Maureen Carlson, Marie Segal, Emi Fukishima, Dotty McMillan and Trina Williams.

My heartfelt gratitude to the marvelous people at North Light Books who have made this experience a lifetime highlight for me: to Greg Albert, thanks for finding me; Catherine Cochran, my marvelous editor and an absolute joy to work with; Christine Polomsky, who made photographing this book a ball; and Jane Friedman, for getting me started.

I'd like to express my appreciation to the ladies of the Las Vegas Polymer Clay Guild, who make the second Monday of every month the most enjoyable night in town! A special thanks to Linda Hirshfield, Helen Soffer, and Melody Stein for keeping me going.

I'd like to extend my gratitude to the following companies who offered their generous support: All Night Media, American Art Clay Company, Artistic Wire, Beads Plus, Clearsnap, Hampton Art Stamps, Inkadinkadoo, Jones Tones, JudiKins, Kemper Tools, The Leather Factory, Manco, The Magnet Source, Polyform Products, Jacquard Products (Rupert, Gibbon & Spider), Personal Stamp Exchange, Sanford, Scratch Art, Stamp Oasis, Toner Plastics and Walnut Hollow.

Last, but certainly not least, the girls who keep me sane: Barbara Berg, Lynne Fletcher, Joy Petitclerc, Audrey Rosenstein, Cheryl Rosenzweig, Debbie Sherwood, "Sister" Linda Steiner, Sue "Model-T" Sullivan and Gayle Weckstein.

contents

polymer clay and

paper crafts
1 ...16

polymer clay and

desk accessories
3 ...56

polymer clay and

memory crafts
2 ...30

polymer clay and

4

polymer clay and

home décor
...90

5

polymer clay and

...76

jewelry

6

...104

garden décor

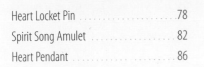

For me, polymer clay was love at first touch!

▶ I remember when I first saw these colorful blocks of clay. I knew they were different from any medium I had experienced before. What amazed me most was how user-friendly it was. It wasn't as unforgiving as two-dimensional mediums such as pencil and paint. Starting over is easy if things don't shape up just the way you like! A little practice and basic knowledge make polymer clay nearly foolproof. Best of all, I found that working with the clay became a form of meditation. It's easy to lose all sense of space and time when working with polymer clay. Hours fly by in what seem like mere seconds. I've often heard that others experience the same phenomenon whenever they sit down to "clay." ▶ The more I worked with it, the more entranced I became. I was astonished at all the materials I could mimic with polymer clay. Like many of my colleagues, I don't hesitate to express the belief that there is no artistic medium as versatile as polymer clay! ▶ This is my first solo book. I wanted to write a book that was accessible to beginners, but would also appeal to more experienced enthusiasts too. The focus of this book is on the projects, with an introductory section for beginners. There are numerous books and websites that go into great depth about working with polymer clay. I saw no need to reinvent the wheel. I've included what I feel is the basic information needed to complete the projects in this book. For those of you who have worked with polymer clay for any length of time, I hope you will pick up some useful tips as well. ▶ A small gallery section of my work and the work of other talented polymer clay artists is included at the end of the book. I hope this section will give you an idea of how versatile this medium truly is. Following the gallery is a resource guide which is an invaluable tool for finding more information on polymer clay and sources for the products used throughout this book. ▶ For me, polymer clay is more than just a hobby. This magical material is a way of life. I have seen the tremendous therapeutic benefits it offers children and adults alike. Polymer clay has opened up careers for many of my friends and me. Most importantly, however, is the fact that it brought many deep and lasting friendships into my life. Whether polymer clay brings significant changes to your life or simply serves as an enjoyable pastime, I hope you share it with friends and family so they too can discover how a little lump of clay can become magic!

▶ Creatively Yours, *Lisa Pavelka*

polymer clay 101

the basics

▲▽

olymer clay is one of the most popular and fastest growing art mediums ever. It isn't traditional clay as we know it. Historically, clay was something obtained from the earth. That was until the introduction of polymer clays well over fifty years ago. Polymer clay is a synthetic modeling compound composed of PVC (Polyvinyl Chloride), color pigments and plasticizer. Unlike earthen clay, polymer clay contains no water and will not dry out or crack during normal preparation. A piece can be worked on for weeks or even months at a time, and with proper storage, polymer clay can have a shelf life of many years. Follow the guidelines on these pages for proper storage, usage and techniques to get the most out of this exciting medium!

working with polymer clay

Polymer clay is such a versatile medium, its possibilities are endless! It can mimic many surfaces from leather, stone and colored glass to wood, fabric, tile and ivory. It can be sculpted, carved, drilled, sanded, rebaked, used as a veneer, molded, painted on or even used like paint! As a low-fired substance, it can be combined with wood, metal, glass, foil, fabric, crystals, cardboard, stone, eggshell and even some heat-resistant plastics for mixed-media applications.

Polymer clay is popular because it appeals both to beginners and advanced artists. It requires no special firing equipment; you simply bake it in a convection or toaster oven at a very low temperature. It's also economical; a little bit goes a long way. Best of all, it offers the user instant gratification.

Choosing Your Clay

There are many brands of polymer clay available, each with its own specific characteristics. Try several brands and you may prefer one over the others. All of the projects in this book are made with Premo Sculpey, which was selected for it's strength and durability.

Premo Sculpey

After curing, Premo is the strongest of the polymer clays. It's very durable and retains flexibility after baking. It is soft enough to be easily conditioned by hand, right out of the package. In addition to a wide assortment of colors, Premo Sculpey offers mica-based metallic and pearlized clays.

Fimo Classic

Another strong clay, Fimo Classic, is often preferred by artists for techniques such as millefiori caning. You may need to use softening agents, along with a dedicated food processor, because of its initial crumbly consistency. It has not dried out, but simply requires more conditioning than some other brands.

Fimo Soft

This clay is easier to condition and work with than Fimo Classic, but it is not as strong after baking. Because of the delicate nature of the projects in this book, I do not recommend using Fimo Soft clay.

Cernit

This clay is very strong after baking. It is the hardest of the polymer clays, but it lacks flexibility. Cured Cernit tends to have a translucent quality, which makes it the preferred clay of doll makers. It is a bit stiff out of the package but responds quickly to the warmth of your hands while conditioning. Cernit clay has a tendency to become overly soft when working with it. Allowing the clay to rest (from handling) for short periods will help firm up the clay.

> **Polymer clay begins to cure at 125° F (52° C).** Do your polymer clay shopping last when running summer errands. Even in 80° F (27° C) temperatures, a car's interior can well exceed 125° F (52° C). Heed this warning, to avoid creating polymer clay building blocks in your car!
>
> **TIP**

Conditioning

All polymer clay needs conditioning to be pliable enough to work with. If not properly conditioned, cured clay may end up brittle in spots and hard in others. Conditioning reintegrates the PVC molecules evenly throughout the plasticizer. Softer clays such as Premo Sculpey can be easily conditioned right out of the package by kneading the clay. Running these clays several times through the largest setting of a pasta machine is also an excellent way to condition clay.

Stiffer clays such as Fimo Classic and Cernit are a bit harder to hand condition. Polyform's Sculpey Diluent and Fimo Mix Quick are softening agents that may be added to clay to help make conditioning easier, but use clay softeners sparingly.

Polymer clay usually becomes stiffer over time. However, most clays, even those stored for years, can be conditioned to a workable consistency. If the clay refuses to condition after you have spent considerable effort, it's possible that the clay has partially cured and is unusable.

> **Always start working with the lightest-colored clays first.** Darker clays can leave a residue on your hands that will contaminate lighter colors handled later. Red clays tend to stain your hands. It's helpful to clean your hands in between colors with a baby wipe. Polymer clay will also pick up any dirt or debris on your hands. A clay-scraping tool available at any art supply store is useful for removing contaminants from the surface of lightly colored clays.
>
> **TIP**

Leaching

Some people find the softer clays difficult to use, especially if they have very warm hands. Leaching is a technique that is used to firm oversoft clay by removing excess plasticizer. To leach clay, roll it through the largest setting of a pasta machine. Sandwich the clay sheet between several layers of copy paper. Stack a flat, heavy object on the top layers of the paper and let the clay sit overnight. The following morning, you'll find that the paper appears to have

an oily stain. This is the plasticizer that has been leached from the clay. Usually doing this procedure once is sufficient to stiffen clay to a more workable consistency. If you find the clay is still too soft, repeat this leaching process one more time.

Measuring

You will need a ruler when measuring the amounts of clay for these projects. You can also find measuring templates designed specifically for polymer clay at craft stores. These templates are helpful when dividing polymer clay blocks and measuring length, diameter and width.

Baking

Polymer clay manufacturers list their recommended baking times and temperatures on the packages. These generally run between 260°–275° F (127°–135° C). The rule of thumb for baking time is fifteen to twenty minutes for every ¼" (6mm) of thickness.

Convection and toaster ovens may all be used to cure polymer clay. Never, ever use a microwave oven for polymer clay! Polymer clay baked in a microwave oven will not cure properly and may burn, creating toxic fumes.

An absolute must-have is an oven thermometer. It can be purchased in most grocery or discount stores. Always preheat and check your oven temperature before placing the clay inside. Ovens often "spike" during the initial heating process, which can cause your clay to burn. Polymer clay doesn't completely harden until cooled. For this reason, it's best not to handle clay while it's still warm.

> **Polymer clay is nontoxic when properly cured.** Burning clay emits toxic fumes, as will any burning plastic. It is not unusual to smell a slight odor when baking polymer clay. If a very strong odor or smoke is detected, turn off the oven, remove the burning clay, ventilate the room and leave the area until the air clears. **SAFETY TIP**

Color Blending

Polymer clay mixes just like paint so kneading colors together will create new colors. Adding white to a color will make it lighter. The more you add, the lighter it will get, so you can custom-blend your own colors. A great tool to create is a chip chart. Glue a baked sample of your custom color to a piece of cardboard. Write formula notations under

each sample for future reference. Organize these charts in a three-ring binder for easy storage.

Blend colors together by hand-kneading or rolling them through the pasta machine until blended. Partially mixing clay will create a beautiful marbled effect that can give projects a sophisticated, textured look.

Storing Polymer Clay

Polymer clay may be stored in wax paper, plastic wrap or a sealable plastic bag. You may also want to organize your clay in plastic containers with compartments. Plastic that can be easily bent and flexed without breaking (polystyrene and nylon) is usually polymer-clay safe. Storage containers made from these plastics will either be semi-opaque or opaque, but never crystal clear. Store polymer clay in a cool area, away from direct light. Properly stored polymer clay can have a very long shelf life.

Work Surfaces

I've found the best work surface is a smooth ceramic tile. It is scratch resistant, comes in many sizes and is very inexpensive. Ceramic tile also works as an excellent baking surface for delicate work that may be damaged if lifted from a work surface to the oven. Items baked directly on a ceramic tile or baking sheet will have shiny spots on the bottom. If a uniform finish is desired, place an index card between the clay and the baking surface.

Once baked, polymer clay is stabilized and will not affect any surface. However, uncured polymer clay should never be placed on painted or lacquered surfaces, as this may damage the finish.

tools

One of the best things about working with polymer clay is that only a few tools are absolutely necessary for most work: a pasta machine, a craft knife and a clay blade are the most essential. Most other tools commonly used with polymer clay are easily obtainable and inexpensive. Below is a list of the basic tools that you should have on hand to complete the projects in this book.

Pasta Machines

Conditioning clay is considerably easier with a pasta machine than kneading it by hand. It enables the user to roll clay into smooth sheets of uniform thickness in mere seconds. Turning the knob on the side of the machine controls the clay thickness. Most machines have six to eight settings, ranging from $1/8$" (3mm) to $1/32$" (0.75mm).

Do not force large balls or thick pieces of clay through the pasta machine, as this may damage the roller's alignment. When conditioning straight from the package, cut a clay block into three or four slices before running it through the pasta machine. When reconditioning stored clay, roll the clay into a 3"–4" (8cm–10cm) snake and flatten it slightly between your hands before running it through a pasta machine.

Softer clays may stick to pasta machine rollers, especially on very thin settings. To help prevent sticking, spray a small amount of automotive protectant onto the rollers and spread it back and forth with your index finger while turning the handle. Clean the pasta machine rollers occasionally with a baby wipe. Dry it with a lint-free rag immediately afterward to prevent rusting.

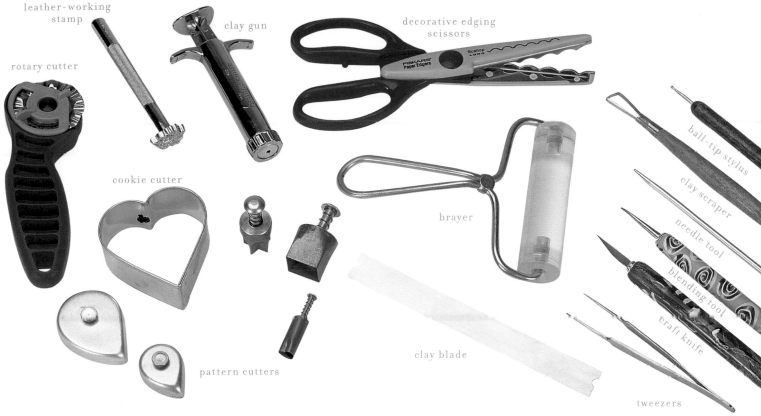

leather-working stamp

clay gun

decorative edging scissors

rotary cutter

ball-tip stylus

clay scraper

needle tool

cookie cutter

blending tool

brayer

craft knife

clay blade

pattern cutters

tweezers

Cutting Tools

Clay blades are the recommended cutting tool for most polymer clay work. They are used for slicing through clay and trimming clay. These blades are extremely sharp and should be used with caution! They are not recommended for use by children.

Identifying the sharp edge of the blade can be tricky. The sharp edge is beveled and can be seen when turning in the light. To make the blade safer to handle, small amounts of scrap clay can be rolled into balls and pressed onto the blunt corners of the blade and baked. After baking, pull the balls off and glue them to the corners with two-part epoxy. A bit of red nail polish can also be painted onto the blunt corners of the blade to make the cutting edge easier to identify.

Blades can lose their sharpness quickly. You can extend the life of your blades by cleaning and sharpening them at the same time. Exercise extreme caution whenever handling the blades and especially when cleaning and sharpening them! Even dull blades are sharp enough to cause severe injury. Cut a small square from a sheet of 800-grit automotive-grade sandpaper. Fold the paper in half, and place the sharp edge of the blade into the folded paper. Carefully slide the paper back and forth along the blade while pinching the paper. Never clean the blade with water. This will cause corrosion.

Periodically inspect the blade edge for notching. Over time, notches will begin to form along the edge. When this occurs, it's time to discard the blade. Proper use, care and storage will extend the life of your blades.

Rolling Tools

Acrylic brayers are helpful in flattening and smoothing clay. Wooden rolling pins may leave unwanted texture in clay. If used, they should be dedicated for clay use only.

Spraying a rolling tool with a silicone-based automotive protectant spray before use will help prevent it from sticking to the clay. **TIP**

Shaping Tools

In addition to basic clay shapers, there are many shaping tools such as pattern cutters, cookie cutters and clay guns that help create wonderful designs in your projects.

Pattern Cutters

These small, punch-type cutters have a spring-loaded plunger to push cut clay from the barrel. They come in various sizes and shapes, including stars, circles, squares, triangles, flowers and teardrops. I used Kemper pattern cutters in many of the projects in this book.

Clay Guns

These devices extrude polymer clay in a variety of shapes and sizes. Clay guns are useful when making borders, braids and hair. To use a clay gun, roll 1/8 block of well-conditioned clay into a 2"–3" (5cm–8cm) snake. Place the clay in the barrel and insert the the plunger to extrude the clay. Because extensive use of a clay gun may cause muscle strain, you may want to also use a bench vice.

Surface Treatments

There are many embellishments and treatments you can use to add to the design of your projects. Experiment with the following techniques to add excitement to your artwork. Just make sure to use one of the sealants on the opposite page after applying any surface treatment to keep it from rubbing off.

Pearlized Powders

Powders are made from ultrafine mica particles. These powders may be brushed over unbaked clay surfaces for a beautiful effect and this effect is enhanced when applied over textured surfaces. The powders come in a large assortment of colors, including interference powders that produce an iridescent effect on clay.

Paint

Cured polymer clay accepts acrylic and water-based paints very well. A beautiful antique effect can be achieved by brushing paint onto textured clay and lightly wiping it away with a damp rag or paper towel, leaving paint embedded in the crevices.

Rubber Stamps

Polymer clay is known for its ability to hold intricate detail. This makes it an ideal candidate for many different methods of adding texture. Using rubber or leather-working stamps on clay is one of the easiest ways to texture it.

Rubber stamps and other items used for texturing may stick to the clay. I recommend using a silicone-based automotive protectant spray. Spray a small amount on the surface of the clay and spread it over the entire surface with your fingers.

It can be difficult to apply deep, even pressure when hand-stamping clay. This can be made easier by laying sprayed clay on top of the stamp and rolling a brayer across the clay's surface. Roll only once, applying firm pressure. Repeated rollings can leave a ghost image in the clay.

Metallic Leafs and Foils

Gold, silver, copper and variegated metallic leaf can be used to create beautiful effects on polymer clay. While these leafs are available in precious metal varieties, the alternate composite (imitation) leaf is much more economical and is virtually indistinguishable from its more expensive counterpart. Metallic leaf is applied to clay prior to baking, and creates a beautiful crackle finish when rolled with a brayer or run through a pasta machine. Fabric foils and mylar-backed foils can also be applied to the clay surface to create the look of dichroic glass.

Glazes, Adhesives & Sealants

When applying any surface treatments such as paint, powder or metallic leaf, a sealer is recommended to protect it. There are several options to choose from when sealing polymer clay surfaces but it's important to select a polymer-clay-safe sealer. Some sealants, especially the aerosol type, may contain solvents that react with the clay and leave a permanently sticky finish.

Clay Glazes

These water-based sealants are available in both gloss and satin. They come in a bottle and must be applied with a brush. Both Polyform and Fimo offer brush-on gloss and matte finishes that are polymer-clay compatible. Beacon Liquid Laminate is an economical water-based sealant that offers a semigloss finish. Blair Sprays are the only aerosols I have found to be polymer-clay compatible. These sprays come in both gloss and matte finishes.

Acrylic Floor Wax

Use acrylic floor wax to achieve a glasslike finish on polished clay. It is very economical and dries in minutes.

Liquid Polymer Clay

This may be brushed on clay before or after baking to seal any surface treatment. Liquid polymer clay is especially useful for protecting metallic foils and image transfers when polishing is intended. It will cure with a milky, semiopaque look. When applied in a thin, even layer, it will become transparent after baking, polishing and glazing. Diluting liquid polymer clay with Polyform Diluent will make it easier to apply thin coats.

Superglue

Superglue is useful in polymer clay work since it bonds clay to clay instantly. The bond is strong enough to fuse clay, but isn't recommended for attaching components that will be frequently handled or worn (like earring and pin backs). I recommend superglue that comes with a brush-on applicator.

Epoxy

Two-part epoxy consists of a resin and an accelerator. The two materials will not bond until mixed. I recommend the five-minute epoxy, which can be found either in syringe or tube form. Syringe epoxy is usually easier to handle because equal amounts of resin and accelerator are extruded when a plunger is depressed. Mix small amounts of epoxy on an index card with a toothpick. Mix both materials well and use it quickly because it begins to set once mixing has started.

Polishing Polymer Clay

Polishing is a wonderful way to give your polymer clay projects a rich finish. Sand baked clay under water with automotive-grade, wet-dry

sandpaper. Start with 600-grit and then follow with 800-grit and then 1000-grit. Buff with a soft 100% cotton or denim cloth for a satin finish.

More experienced polymer clay artists may want to invest in a muslin buffing wheel. However, not every muslin wheel will polish clay. In fact, some will scratch it. Look for a loose-weave wheel, made especially for polishing. Hold the piece tightly in your hands and buff it lightly against the wheel, rotating it every few seconds. You will notice the shine begin to rise on the clay's surface. For a glasslike finish, add a light coat of acrylic floor wax on the polished clay.

When buffing on a wheel, always wear protective eyewear and a dustmask.

SAFETY TIP

CLEAN-UP

Proper care and maintenance of your tools will help them last for many years.

▼ *Carefully disassemble your pasta machine and clean any residual clay with rubbing alcohol. Do not immerse any part of it in water.*

▼ *To clean a clay gun, bake it at 270° F (132° C) for ten minutes. When the gun is cool, scrape the hardened clay out with a needle tool.*

▼ *Use Polyform Diluent to clean brushes used for liquid polymer clay. Pour a few drops into the bristles and wipe well with a paper towel.*

▼ *Use a waterless hand cleanser with pumice to remove the waxlike residue clay leaves on your hands.*

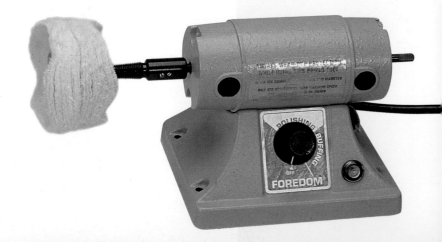

basic techniques

Now that you have a general understanding of polymer clay and the tools and materials, two basic techniques are important to learn before you begin many of the projects. They are Skinner Blend and Millefiori caning. Use these techniques to give your projects a level of sophistication and style. They may look complicated, but you will be amazed at how simple they really are!

Skinner Blend Cane

This technique was developed by polymer clay pioneer Judith Skinner to combine two or more colors to create a graduated color blend. Several of the projects in this book call for simple, two-tone Skinner Blend canes. Refer to the instructions in this chapter using the colors specified when a Skinner Blend is required.

1 Condition ½ block of each color and cut a 3" x 3" (8cm x 8cm) square with a clay blade. Cut each square in an offset triangle by lining the blade ⅛" (3mm) from the diagonal. Cut through the square with the blade. Repeat this process for the second color.

2 Stack the two triangular halves over each other. Piece the double-thick triangles together to form a square.

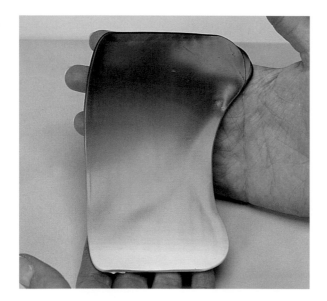

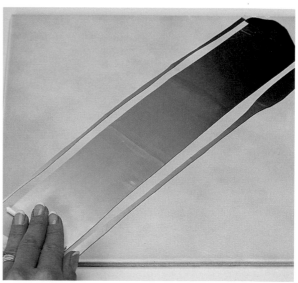

3 Run this square through the largest setting of the pasta machine. Fold the clay in half, white to white and black to black. Repeat rolling it through the largest setting of the pasta machine 25–30 times until a graduated blend is achieved.

4 Roll the clay four more times through the pasta machine, reducing the thickness setting with each pass. Set the stretched sheet on the work surface and trim the clay to a long rectangle.

caning TIPS

▼ *Reduce canes by gently squeezing from the center and rotating. Continue this motion while working out towards one end of the cane. Repeat this step for the other half of the cane.*

▼ *Further reduction of a cane can also be achieved by rolling the cane by hand and stretching it. Use a brayer for square and triangular canes.*

▼ *Cut thin, even slices by looking down directly over the clay blade when cutting.*

5 Roll up the clay jelly-roll style. Wrap the cane in a sheet of clay the same color as the outer color, rolled through the fourth-largest setting of the pasta machine. Trim excess clay with a clay blade.

6 Cut thin, even slices with a clay blade. Canes are very soft after construction, so allow them to rest one or two days before slicing or firm them up quickly by placing them in the freezer for 10–15 minutes.

Millefiori Caning

Millefiori caning is adapted from an ancient Roman glassblowing method. The process is used to create patterns in a length of clay by combining sheets and snakes of polymer clay. The term in Italian literally means *"a thousand flowers"*. Geometric, flower and pictorial patterns are commonly constructed in millefiori caning. Here are instructions for a flower pattern.

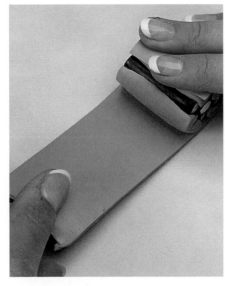

1 Create an image using several Skinner blend canes and clay snakes. Pack the sections of the canes very tightly. Air pockets will distort the pattern in the millefiori cane.

2 Wrap the canes and snakes in a sheet of clay that has been run through the fourth-largest setting of the pasta machine. Again, make sure there are no air bubbles.

3 Roll the millefiori cane out to your desired diameter. Let the cane rest for a few hours before cutting thin slices.

polymer clay and paper crafts

Greeting cards have come a long way in the last couple of decades.

They are no longer the simple, two-dimensional cards of the past. Mixing polymer clay with other mediums is a great way to turn simple greeting cards into truly artistic expressions. This time-honored method of communicating is now multidimensional, inspiring and suitable for framing! Using rubber stamps, wire and iridescent powders, you can make what was once mundane and ordinary, into something extraordinary! More than just a card, these projects are a gift within a card.

Love Magnet
card

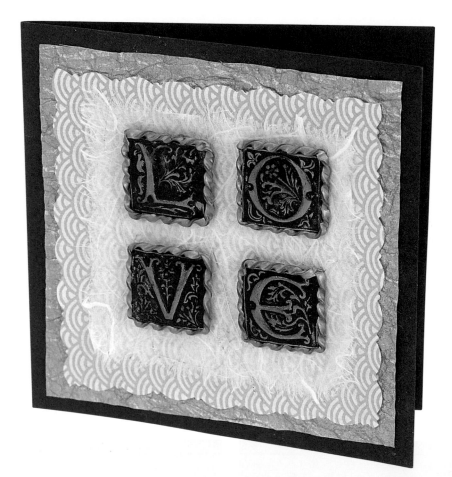

t his card is perfect for Valentine's Day or just to say
"I love you" anytime of the year. Combine polymer
clay and rubber stamping to create this one-of-a-kind
project. Iridescent powders highlight the raised letters of
this multilayered card. Expect this card to stick around.
Recipients of this card can detach the L-O-V-E magnets
and put them on the refrigerator or filing cabinet to show
they're lucky in love.

materials

- polymer clay
  - 1 black block
  - 1 gold block
- gold pearlized powder
- L-O-V-E rubber stamp set
- 11" x 5½" (28cm x 14cm) black cardstock
- 5" x 5" (13cm x 13cm) piece of gold crinkle paper
- 4½" x 4½" (11cm x 11cm) gold scallop paper
- 4" x 4" (10cm x 10cm) white mulberry paper with gold flecks

- decorative edging scissors
- adhesive-backed magnetic sheeting
- double-sided adhesive
- matte acrylic spray sealer
- poster tack
- superglue
- cotton swabs
- eye shadow applicator (optional)

1 Stamp and Trim the Block Letters

Roll out the black clay on the third-largest setting of the pasta machine. Lightly spray the clay with automotive protectant and spread it with your fingers. Stamp the L-O-V-E letters into the clay. Cut out the letter squares along the stamped markings with a craft knife. Remove the excess clay.

2 Add Gold Accents

With either the tip of your finger or an eye shadow applicator, apply gold pearlized powder on the raised area of the stamped letters.

3 Create a Twisted Border

Roll ⅛ block of gold clay into a 5" (13cm) snake and run it through the pasta machine on the fourth-largest setting. Trim the clay sheet to 5" x 1" (13cm x 3cm) with a clay blade. Cut four strips ⅛" (3mm) wide and twist.

4 Glue the Border to the Letters

Brush superglue along one side of each letter and gently press the twisted strip against the clay's edge. Continue gluing the border around the entire letter, wrapping all four sides. Trim the excess clay with a craft knife. Repeat this step for the remaining three letters. Bake the letters at 270 °F (132° C)) for twenty-five minutes, then let it cool.

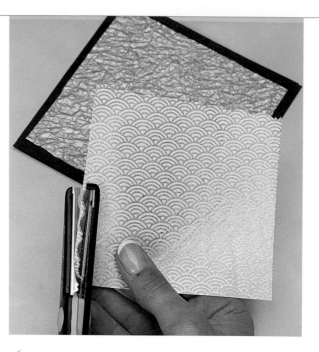

5 Make the Card Background

While the letters are in the oven, score and fold the 11" x 5½" (28cm x 14cm) sheet of black cardstock in half. Apply double-sided adhesive to the 5" x 5" (13cm x 13cm) piece of gold crinkle paper and attach it to the cardstock.

6 Add the Scalloped-Edged Paper

Trim a piece of gold scallop-pattern paper with decorative edging scissors to 4½" x 4½" (11cm x 11cm). Apply double-sided adhesive and center it over the gold crinkle paper.

7 Dampen the Mulberry Paper

Dip a cotton swab into water. Wet the outer edges of the 4"x 4" (10cm x 10cm) mulberry paper with the dampened swab.

8 Create a Feathered Edge

Gently grasp the mulberry paper in one hand. Tear away the dampened edges of the paper. This will leave a feathered edge.

10 Add Magnetic Sheeting to the Letters

Loosen the cooled letters from the tile with a clay blade. Cut four ⅛" x ⅛" (2cm x 2cm) squares from an adhesive-backed magnetic sheet. Peel off the adhesive backing and superglue them to the adhesive side for extra hold. Press the magnets onto the back of each letter. Lightly spray the letters with the acrylic spray sealer to seal the powder, and let them dry.

9 Add the Mulberry Paper to the Card

Apply double-sided adhesive to one side of the feathered paper. Center the mulberry paper and place it on top of the scallop paper.

11 Attach the Letters to the Card

Apply a small ball of poster tack to the back of each letter. Arrange the letters on the mulberry paper as shown on the finished card.

> **Don't let all of your work be in vain!** Send polymer clay cards in padded envelopes. Also, mark both sides of the envelope, "Please Hand Cancel." Automated canceling may damage the card.
>
> # TIP

Snowman Ornament
card

*d*on't just send a card, send a greeting card and keepsake ornament—all in one! This cheerful little snowman can be detached from the card to brighten any tree or holiday display. Not just another card to be taped to the door, this fanciful ornament is sure to be found hanging on a tree throughout the entire holiday season. Don't be surprised if everyone on your holiday card list keeps this snowman as an heirloom ornament for years to come.

materials

- polymer clay

  1 black block
  1 green block
  1 orange block
  1 red block
  1 white block
  1 yellow block

- small star (PC5S) pattern cutter

- 7" x 11" (18cm x 28cm) piece of gold cardstock

- 5" x 6½" (13cm x 17cm) piece of holly-pattern paper

- 5" x 6" (13cm x 15cm) piece of red mulberry paper with gold flecks

- 18" (46cm) green plastic-coated craft wire

- pink blush

- decorative edge scissors

- double-sided adhesive

- poster tack

- scouring pad

- tracing paper

- eye shadow appliator

- craft knife

- cotton swabs

- ball-tip stylus

- large-gauge knitting needle

- needle-nose pliers

- needle tool

Use this template for the Snowman Ornament Card

1 Add Texture and Rosy Cheeks

Roll out a block of white clay on the largest setting of your pasta machine and using the template and a craft knife, create the snowman. Pat a kitchen scouring pad over the surface of the snowman to texture. Finally, apply dots of blush to the snowman's cheeks with an eye shadow applicator.

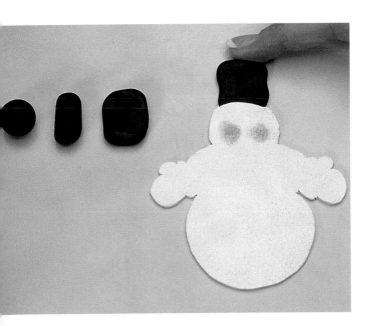

2 Create the Top Hat

Roll a ⅝" (2cm) ball of black clay into a 1⅛" (3cm) snake. Flatten and shape the snake into a "scrunchy" rectangle with your fingers to create a crown. Press the crown over the top edge of the head.

3 Add the Brim of the Hat

Roll a ⅝" (2cm) ball of black clay into a 1⅛" (3cm) snake. Slightly flatten the snake and indent the center with your fingertip to make the brim of the hat. Press the brim over the base of the crown.

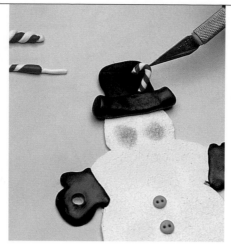

4 Create the Mittens and Buttons

Roll ⅛ of a block of black clay through the third-largest setting of a pasta machine and cut out the mittens using the template on page 23. Use a needle tool to make holes in the center of each mitten. Next, roll two pinches of green clay into tiny balls for buttons and press them onto the center of the snowman's torso. Slightly flatten the balls with your fingertip. Poke two holes into the center of each button with a needle tool.

5 Make the Candy Cane

Roll pinches of white and red clay into very thin snakes (work with the white first). Clean your hands thoroughly after using the red clay. Twist the snakes together. Roll them against the work surface until they are smooth and ⅛" (3mm) in diameter. Bend the top 1" (3cm) of the candy cane into a hook and press it onto the hat, above the brim.

6 Add a Gold Star

Roll a pinch of yellow clay through the fifth-largest setting of the pasta machine. Cut out a star with the pattern cutter. Press the star over the bottom of the candy cane to secure it to the hat.

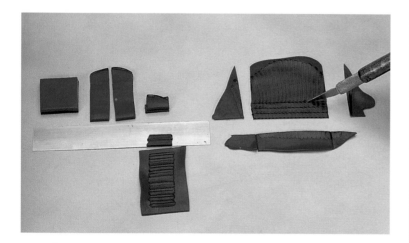

7 Make a Patterned Scarf

Roll ⅛ block of black and ⅛ block of red clay through the largest setting of the pasta machine. Stack the clay sheets and trim with a clay blade to make a 1" x 1" (3cm x 3cm) square. Roll this square through the third-largest setting of the pasta machine. Cut this sheet in half and stack these halves together, alternating colors. Roll ⅟₁₆ block of red clay through the fifth-largest setting of the pasta machine. Cut six ⅛" (3mm) slices from the stack. Lay these slices, side-by-side, over the red clay sheet. Run this sheet, stripes facing up, through the fourth-largest setting of the pasta machine. Cut two 2" x ¼" (5cm x 6mm) strips from the striped sheet.

8 Add the Scarf to the Snowman

Wrap the first striped strip around the snowman's neck and cut the excess away. Fold the second strip at a right angle. Place the folded strip over the right side of the scarf to form the tails. Trim scarf tails at an angle with a craft knife.

9 Add the Carrot Nose and Coal Eyes

Roll a pinch of orange clay into a long teardrop. Bend the teardrop with your fingers to create a crooked carrot. Place the carrot, pointed end down, at an angle between the cheeks. Mark lines along the length of the carrot with the tip of a craft knife. Make two indentations over the cheeks with a ball-tip stylus. Roll two tiny pinches of black clay into balls. Press the balls into the holes. Bake the snowman at 270° F (132° C) for thirty minutes.

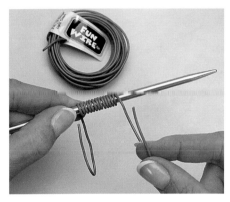

10 Coil the Wire

Allow the snowman to cool completely. Bend the 18" (46cm) piece of green wire in half over a large knitting needle. Wrap each end around the knitting needle six times (for a total of twelve coils). Bend the remaining lengths of wire in half to form a long U shape. Slide the wire off the knitting needle. Holding the wire coiled at both ends, slightly pull it apart with your fingers and bend it in an arch.

11 Add the Wire to the Snowman

Slip the U-shaped hooks through the mitten holes. With needle-nose pliers, twist the ends of each wire two to three times around the wire extending from the coil.

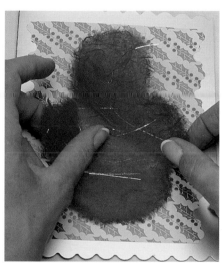

12 Construct the Card

Fold a piece of gold cardstock in half and trim the top and bottom edges with decorative edging scissors, creating a 5½" x 7" (14cm x 18cm) card. Trim the holly-pattern paper with decorative edging scissors to 5" x 6¼" (13cm x 16cm). Create an outline of the snowman by feathering the edge of the mulberry paper, about ½" (1cm) from edge of the snowman. See steps 7 and 8 on page 20 for further instruction. Attach these three pieces with double-sided adhesive to make the card.

13 Attach the Ornament to the Card

Apply four to five small balls of poster tack to the back of the snowman. Press the snowman over the center of the mulberry paper to secure the ornament to the card.

Mother & Child
scrapbook

Some of the most precious memories in a person's life are those that capture special moments between a mother and her child. This beautiful scene is the ideal focal point for transforming a small scrapbook or photo album into a treasured keepsake. Hand-tooled metal is the centerpiece of this artful scrapbook cover. The mother and child in repose are framed by a stamped clay background and millefiori border. This unique project is a touching tribute to cherished mother-and-child memories.

materials

- polymer clay
  - 1 black block
  - 1 cobalt blue block
  - 1 pearl block
  - 1 ultramarine blue block
- liquid polymer clay
- silver metal emboss sheet
- 3½" x 3½" mother & child rubber stamp
- black pigment stamp pad
- leaves rubbing plate
- 7"x 5" (18cm x x13cm) blue scrapbook
- automotive protectant
- black permanent markers— fine and very fine
- epoxy
- superglue
- 1 sheet lightweight cardboard
- acrylic rod or brayer
- ball-tip stylus
- small-gauge knitting needle
- needle tool
- paintbrush

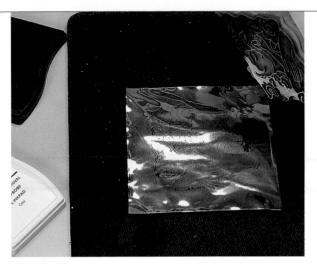

1 Stamp the Metal Emboss Sheet

Cut a 4" x 4" (10cm x 10cm) square of the metal emboss sheet. Ink the stamp and apply it to the sheet. Let the sheet dry for five minutes.

2 Outline the Stamp with a Stylus

Move the stamped metal to a mouse pad or an open page of a telephone book. Indent the stamped lines with the small end of a ball-tip stylus. Use the tip of a needle tool to indent the fine lines in the pattern.

3 Fill In the Back with Liquid Polymer Clay

Turn over the embossed metal (red side up). Squeeze out a generous amount of liquid polymer clay. Spread the liquid over the embossed design with a brush. Continue adding liquid polymer clay until all the recessed areas are filled. There should be enough liquid polymer clay to create a level backing on the embossed plate. This prevents the design from being crushed. Bake the plate at 275° F (135° C) for thirty minutes.

4 Color and Outline the Stamp

After the metal has cooled, darken the indented lines with permanent markers.

If markers stop working, stroke them a few times across a piece of white paper until the ink flow resumes. TIP

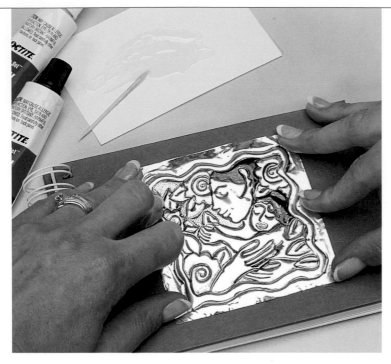

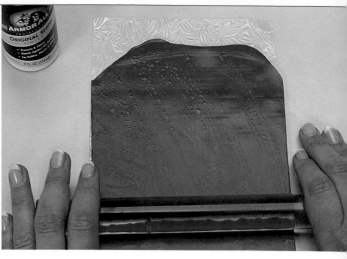

5 Attach the Metal Sheet to the Scrapbook Cover

Mix a generous amount of two-part epoxy on an index card. Spread the epoxy over the back of the metal plate and press it onto the center of the scrapbook cover.

6 Make a Clay Border for the Metal Sheet

Roll a block of ultramarine blue clay into a 5" (13cm) long snake. Roll this snake through the third-largest setting on the pasta machine. Set this sheet over a piece of white paper on the work surface. Spray the clay sheet with automotive protectant and spread it with your fingers. Place the sprayed clay sheet over the leaves rubbing plate. Roll an acrylic rod or brayer over the clay, pressing firmly. Make only one pass over the textured sheet; repeated rolling will create shadow impressions in the clay.

7 Cut the Clay to Fit the Scrapbook

Cut a 6" x 4½" (15cm x 11cm) piece of cardboard and lay it over the embossed ultramarine blue clay. Cut around the template edges with a clay blade.

8 Create a Frame

Cut a 3½" x 3½" (9cm x 9cm) square of cardboard and center it over the embossed clay. Cut around the template and remove the excess of the clay in the center.

9 Glue the Clay to the Scrapbook

Mix a generous amount of epoxy and spread it around the outside edge of the metal plate. Carefully lift the blue clay frame and place it over the metal plate on the scrapbook cover. Add more epoxy, if needed, under the edges and corners of the blue clay.

10 Create a Border Around the Frame

Make a light blue pearl clay by mixing a block of pearl and a ⅝" (2cm) ball of cobalt blue clay. Make a light blue pearl and cobalt blue Skinner Blend following the instructions on page 14. Cut a 1" (3cm) section from the Skinner Blend cane. Wrap this section with a sheet of black clay rolled through the third-largest setting of the pasta machine. Press a small-gauge knitting needle along the top length of the cane, pushing two thirds of the way through the cane. Remove the knitting needle and press the separated halves together. Roll and reduce the cane to 4" (10cm) long. Align the cane so that the black center line faces up from the bottom at each end. Pinch the top portion of the cane between thumb and index finger, along the entire length, to form a leaf shape. Superglue these slices in a scallop fashion around the outer border of the blue clay.

Allow the cane to rest or freeze for fifteen minutes before slicing. Cut several dozen ¹⁄₁₆" (1.5mm) thick slices. Flip the cane back and forth with each cut to keep from distorting the leaf shape. **TIP**

11 Create the Inside Border for the Frame

Roll a ¾" (2cm) ball of light blue pearl clay into a 15" (38cm) snake, ³⁄₁₆" (5mm) diameter. Starting at one corner, superglue the snake around the inside edge of the blue clay frame. Cut off the excess clay.

12 Add Final Touches

Mark indented lines around the light blue clay border every ¼" (6mm) with the tip of the needle tool. Bake the scrapbook at 270° F (132° C) for thirty minutes.

polymer clay and memory crafts

People all over the world have rediscovered the joy of tracing their family roots and preserving family memories.

Creative techniques for displaying precious family memories can take you beyond traditional scrapbooking. You can highlight mementos of the past and the present by showcasing them with polymer clay. Adding artistic elements such as beading, rubber-stamping and wire work create unique ways to display your most treasured moments. These hand-crafted creations will themselves become the heirlooms of the future.

Heart
photo holder

In the mood for a picture frame alternative? You've probably seen wire photo holders popping up in stores all over. Why not make your own? Use the Skinner Blend technique, featured on page 14, to create shaded hearts combined with twisted wire to create a space-saving and fanciful way to display three of your cherished photos.

materials

- polymer clay

    1 copper block
    1 white block
    1 blue pearl block

- 4' (1.2m) blue plastic-coated
  18-gauge wire

- epoxy

- ball-tip stylus
- clay blade
- needle tool
- wire cutters

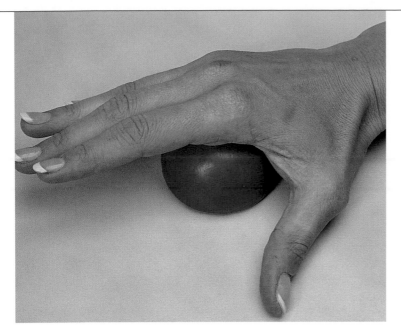

1 Make the Photo Base

Roll a block of blue pearl clay into a ball. Cup the palm of your hand and place it over the ball, slightly flattening it against the work surface.

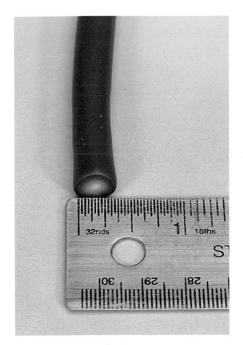

2 Create a Skinner Blend Cane

Make a white and copper Skinner Blend cane. Cut and reduce one half to ³⁄₈" (1cm) in diameter. For detailed instructions on Skinner Blends see pages 14–15 in the Basic Techniques section.

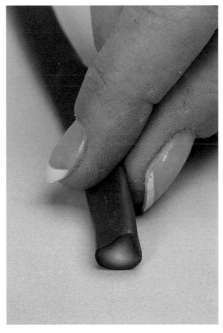

3 Form a Teardrop Shape

Between your thumb and index finger, pinch the reduced cane along its length to form a teardrop shape.

4 Form the Hearts

Trim away the ends and cut the cane in half. Press the two cane sections together, pointed ends down. Let the cane rest or freeze for fifteen minutes. Slice sixteen ¹⁄₁₆" (2mm) thick slices from the heart cane with a clay blade.

5 Create the Center Design

Center four of the cane hearts on the top of the blue clay base. The pointed tips of each heart should meet in the middle. Press the cane slices firmly into place.

6 Surround the Base with Hearts

Press four more cane slices (pointed ends down) directly opposite the four hearts on the top of the base.

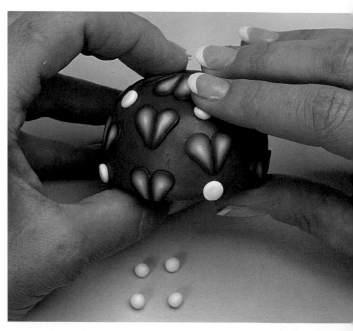

7 Continue Adding Hearts

Press the next four cane slices between and slightly below the first row of four hearts. Press the last four cane slices between and slightly below the second row of hearts. Cut the overhanging tips of the cane hearts flush with the bottom of the photo holder base.

8 Add Decorative Dots

Roll 1/8 block of white clay into a snake 1/4" (6mm) in diameter. Cut nine 1/8" (3mm) sections from the snake and roll into balls. Press eight of the white balls over the top and bottom of the hearts in the second row. Make sure each ball is centered between the hearts, leaving blue clay showing around each dot.

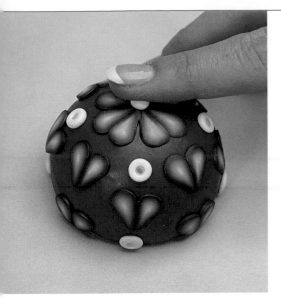

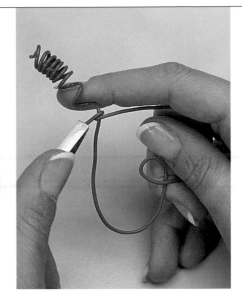

9 Impress the Decorative Dots

Indent the center of each white clay ball with the small end of a ball-tip stylus. Press the final dot in the center of the top four joined hearts and impress with the stylus. This center dot, along with the two on either side, will anchor the wire for the photo holder.

10 Coil the Wire

Cut the blue coated wire into two 12" (30cm) sections and one 16" (40cm) section with wire cutters. Form a tail by bending the last ½" (1cm) of the end of the wire. Then wrap the wire around the handle of a needle tool eight times.

11 Make the Wire Hearts

Bend the remaining wire into a heart, as shown. Finish the end by wrapping it around the base of the wire heart three or four times to secure. Repeat this step with two 12" (30cm) sections of wire, coiling the wire around the needle tool three times.

12 Add Final Touches

Pull the coils slightly apart and bend the wire tails so that they point downward from the coils. Insert the large wire heart into the white center dot at the top of the base. Insert the two smaller wire hearts into white dots on either side of the center ball. Bake at 270° F (132° C) for one hour. Allow the baked holder to cool before adjusting the wires and adding the photos. To strengthen the holder, carefully pull the wires out of the cooled photo holder and reinsert with a bit of epoxy applied to the ends.

Tooth Fairy
box

d oes the Tooth Fairy keep waking up the little ones when she visits? There's a better way to set out those special baby teeth for her. This delightful box will safely hold that prized tooth until the Tooth Fairy finds her way to your child's room. No more digging under the pillow for teeth or money that falls out from under the pillow at night. You'll learn a technique for using fabric foil to make those polymer clay stars really shine! Simple sculpting basics turn an ordinary papier-mâché box into a keepsake, ideal for containing all those baby teeth until the last one falls out!

materials

- polymer clay

  1 beige block
  1 black block
  1 blue pearl block
  1 gold block

- acrylic paint

  1 blue pearl
  1 gold pearl

- gold fabric foil

- gold leaf foil

- embossing heat gun (or hair dryer)

- medium (K46) leaf pattern cutter

- small (PC5S) and medium (PC4S) star pattern cutters

- 2" (5cm) diameter circle cookie cutter

- small star papier-mâché box

- epoxy

- 1 large pearl-head quilting pin

- pink blush

- superglue

- straight pin

- art sponge

- ball-tip stylus

- craft knife

- eye shadow applicator

- wire cutters

- polymer clay glaze-gloss (optional)

1 Paint the Papier-Mâché Box

Paint the papier-mâché box and lid with two coats of blue pearl acrylic paint. Once it has dried, sponge on the gold pearl acrylic paint. To do this, first wet the sponge and squeeze out the excess water. Dip the moistened sponge into the gold paint and dab over the painted surface of the box and lid.

2 Add Gold Foil to the Gold Clay

While the box is drying, roll ¼ block of gold clay through the third-largest setting of pasta machine. Cut a 4"x 4" (10cm x 10cm) square of gold fabric foil and place it over the clay.

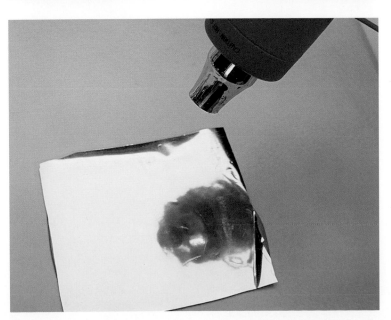

3 Burnish the Clay

Rub your fingers back and forth over the foil to burnish the clay. Hold a heat gun or hair dryer 6"–8" (15cm–20cm) away from the foil for four to five seconds. Do not overheat or the clay will begin to cure, making it unworkable. While the foil is still warm, burnish it once again by vigorously rubbing the front side of a metal ruler over the foil.

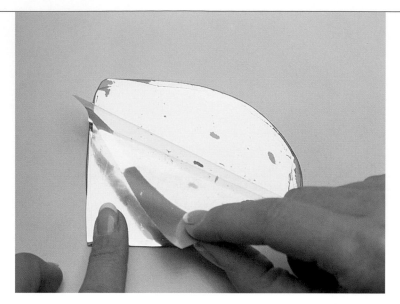

4 Remove the Foil

Immediately after burnishing, lift a corner of the foil and tear it away quickly. The faster you pull, the better the results. There may be spots where the foil doesn't stick to the clay. The foil can be reburnished before you continue.

5 Punch Out the Stars

Cut out about thirty stars with both the small and medium pattern cutters. Superglue the stars randomly over the painted lid and box. Save the remaining foiled clay for the Tooth Fairy's headband in step 18.

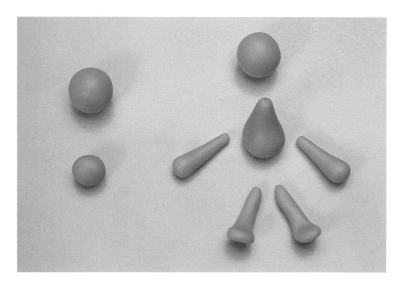

6 Begin Constructing the Tooth Fairy

For the head, roll a $5/8$" (2cm) ball of beige clay. Next, for the torso, roll a $5/8$" (2cm) ball of beige clay into a teardrop shape. For the arms and legs, roll four $7/16$" (1cm) balls of beige clay into 1" (3cm) long teardrops. Slightly flatten the large ends of two teardrops between your thumb and index finger. Bend the flattened ends at a 90° angle to form feet. Press the pointed ends of the legs onto the bottom of the teardrop body.

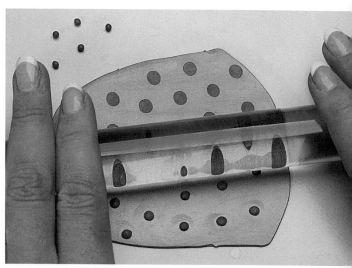

7 Make Polka-Dotted Clay

Roll $1/4$ block of gold clay through the fourth-largest setting of the pasta machine. Roll approximately fifteen tiny balls of pearl blue clay. Press the balls onto the flattened gold clay. Embed the balls into the clay with an acrylic brayer or roller.

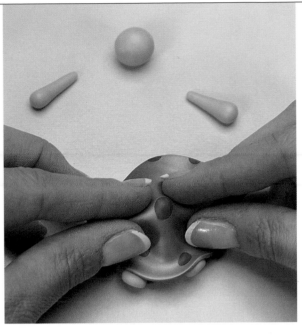

8 Create the Tooth Fairy's Dress

Cut out a 2" (5cm) circle from the polka-dotted clay with the circle cookie cutter. This will become the Tooth Fairy's dress.

9 Cover the Torso with the Dress

Drape the dress over the top of the body and shape it with your fingers.

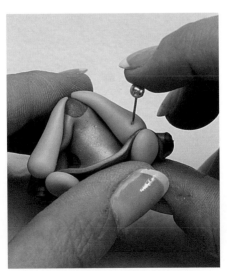

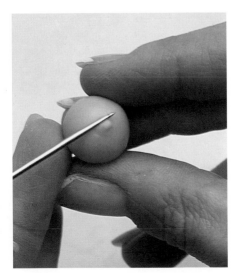

10 Add the Tooth Fairy's Arms

Press the pointed end of the teardrop arms over the dress on either side of the Tooth Fairy's neck.

11 Add the Magic Wand

Cut the pointed tip off the pearl head quilting pin with wire cutters. Insert the pin through one of the Tooth Fairy's hands and into her body to create her magic wand.

12 Add Her Nose

Press a tiny ball of beige clay onto the head for the nose. Blend the outer edges of the nose onto the face with a ball-tip stylus.

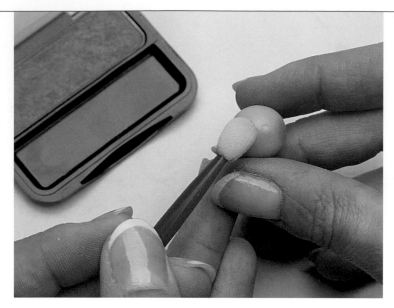

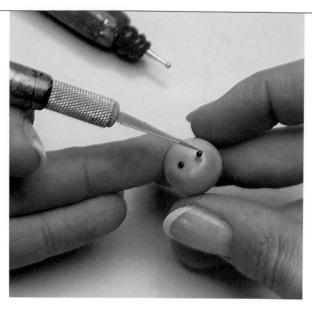

13 Apply Blush to the Tooth Fairy's Cheeks

Apply small dots of pink blush on either side of the nose with an eye shadow applicator.

14 Add the Tooth Fairy's Eyes

Press the small end of a ball-tip stylus into the face twice above the cheeks for the eyes. Roll two tiny balls of black clay and insert them into the holes for the eyes.

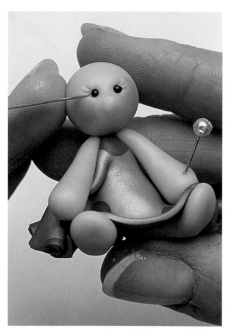

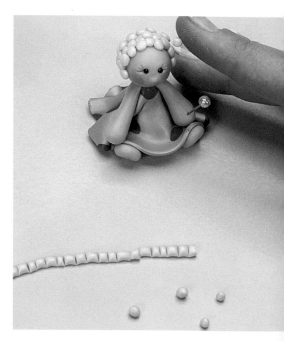

15 Attach the Head

Cut the head off a straight pin with wire cutters. Insert the pin halfway into the top of the Tooth Fairy's body. Press the head over the exposed pin and onto the body.

16 Create Eyelashes

Once the head is securely attached to the body, press the tip of a needle tool above each eye two or three times to create eyelashes.

17 Create the Tooth Fairy's Hair

Roll a large ball of pearl clay into a snake 1/8" (3mm) in diameter. Cut several dozen tiny sections from the snake with the craft knife. Roll these sections into balls and press all over the head to make the hair.

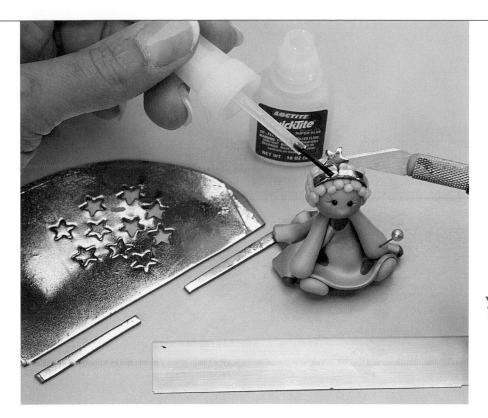

18 Add Her Headband

Cut a ¾" x ⅛" (19mm x 3mm) section from the left-over foiled clay. Superglue this strip over the hair, just beyond the bangs. Punch a small star from the foiled clay and superglue it onto the headband.

> **Give the Tooth Fairy's** eyes a little extra sparkle by dotting them with a stylus dipped into polymer clay glaze gloss finish.
>
> # TIP

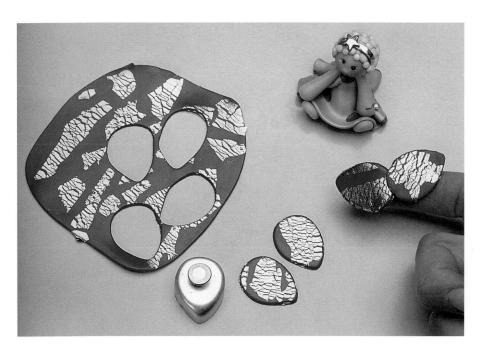

19 Create the Tooth Fairy's Wings

Roll ¼ block blue pearl clay through the largest setting of the pasta machine. Tear fragments from a sheet of gold leaf foil and place them randomly over the blue clay. Roll the blue clay through the third-largest setting of the pasta machine. Cut four teardrop shapes from the foiled sheet with a leaf cutter. Overlap the large ends of the teardrops and press them together. Repeat this with the two remaining teardrops. Press these two joined sections together with the edges overlapping.

20 Add Final Touches

Superglue the wings, foil facing forward, to the back of the Tooth Fairy. Bake at 270° F (132° C) for thirty minutes. When the Tooth Fairy is cool, glue her to the box lid with two-part epoxy.

Vintage Gilded
frame

*P*icture frames can be costly, especially the gilded variety. With a few simple tools and a bit of clay, you can quickly create a lovely frame to show off that treasured photo. In this project, you will learn the steps for making a simple easel frame. Rubber-stamping and mica-based powders are combined with clay to make an elegant showpiece that highlights your handiwork.

materials

- polymer clay
  - 1 black block
  - 2 gold blocks
- gold leaf foil
- gold pearlized powder
- field of flowers rubber stamp (I used Judikins Origami Background Stamp)
- black pigment rubber stamp pad
- 2¾" (7cm) heart cookie cutter

- double-sided adhesive
- matte acrylic spray
- 2 sheets 8½" x 11" (xxcm x xxcm) lightweight cardboard
- superglue
- ball-tip stylus
- craft knife
- ruler
- flat paint brush

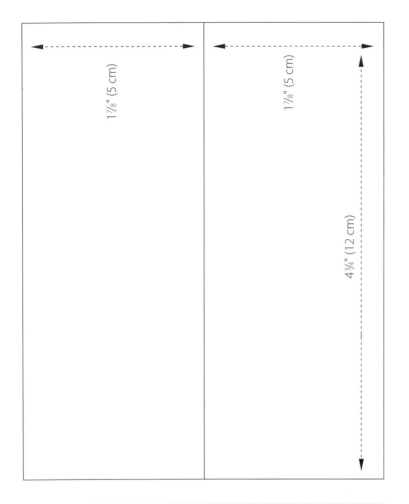

1⁷⁄₈" (5 cm)

1⁷⁄₈" (5 cm)

4³⁄₄" (12 cm)

Use this template for the Vintage Gilded Frame

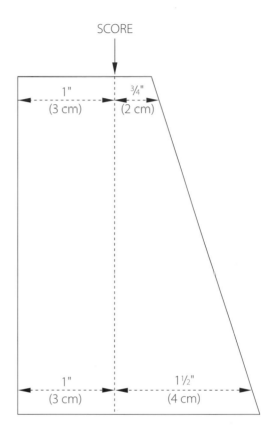

SCORE

1"
(3 cm)

³⁄₄"
(2 cm)

1"
(3 cm)

1½"
(4 cm)

1 Create a Gilded Finish

Roll one block of gold clay through the largest setting of the pasta machine. Lay the clay sheet on a ceramic tile. Cover the surface of the clay with gold pearlized powder, using a dry paint brush.

2 Stamp the Gold Clay

Ink the rubber stamp and impress the clay. Apply enough pressure to leave a deep impression. Your finished frame will measure 4" x 5" (10cm x 13cm), so be sure your stamp covers a large enough surface.

3 Trim the Stamped Clay

With a clay blade, trim the clay to 4" x 5" (10cm x 13cm). Then, cut out an opening from the center of the clay with a 2¾" (7cm) wide heart-shaped cookie cutter and remove the excess clay.

4 Create the Foiled Border

Roll ¼ block of black clay into a 5" (13cm) snake. Wrap the snake in a sheet of gold leaf. Cut away any excess leaf foil. Roll the foiled clay into a 20" (51cm) snake, ⅜" (1cm) in diameter.

5 Glue the Outside Border

Superglue the snake around the outside edges of the stamped clay. Press the foiled snake firmly against the glued edges to secure. Trim the excess clay.

6 Add the Inside Border

Roll the remaining foiled clay snake into a 10" (25cm) snake ⅛" (3mm) in diameter. Superglue this snake to the inside edge of the heart opening. Cut off the excess clay and bake the frame on the tile at 270° F (132° C) for thirty minutes. When the baking is complete, allow the frame to cool.

7 Create the Easel Backing

Cut out the cardboard backing of the frame with a craft knife, following the outside edge of the template provided on page 43. On the easel backing, score from the top to the bottom points of the score line with a ruler and a ball-tip stylus. Fold at the score line. Apply double-sided adhesive aligning the bottom of the glued section with the center and the bottom of the frame backing.

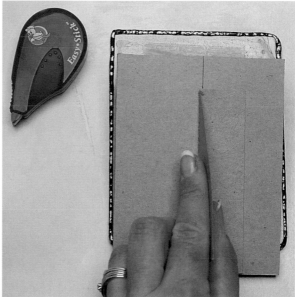

8 Add Final Touches

Lightly spray the cooled clay with matte acrylic spray. When dry, center your chosen photo behind the heart-shaped opening of the cooled frame and apply double-sided adhesive to the backing and attach it to the frame.

Mini Photo
album

don't leave home without them! Take those cherished photos of family and friends everywhere you go with this miniature photo album. This project is especially fitting for those who like to travel light! You'll learn a simple bookbinding technique to tuck six mini photos into your purse or pocket. Rubber-stamping and ribbon round out this adorable project. Jewelry findings may also be added to fashion a unique brooch or pendant.

materials

- polymer clay

  1 gold block
  1 fuchsia block
  1 purple block
  1 turquoise block

- gold leaf foil

- small (PC5H) and medium (PC4H) heart pattern cutters

- leaf pattern rubber stamp

- 2 pieces of ⅛" (3mm) purple satin ribbon, 5" (13cm) long

- white cardstock

- automotive protectant

- double-sided carpet tape (from home improvement or hardware store)

- clay blade

- knitting needle

- scissors

- superglue

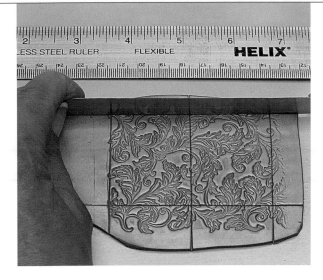

1 Create the Book Cover

Roll ¼ block of gold clay through the third-largest setting on the pasta machine. Spray automotive protectant on the clay sheet and spread it with your fingers. Stamp the clay sheet with the leaf stamp. Cut two 1½"x 2" (4cm x 5cm) covers from the stamped clay with a clay blade.

2 Make the Foiled Hearts

Roll large balls of purple, turquoise and fuchsia clay through the largest setting of the pasta machine. Tear bits of gold leaf foil and apply them over the flattened clay. Run the foiled clays through the fourth-largest setting of the pasta machine. Punch out six hearts, two of each color, using the medium heart pattern cutter.

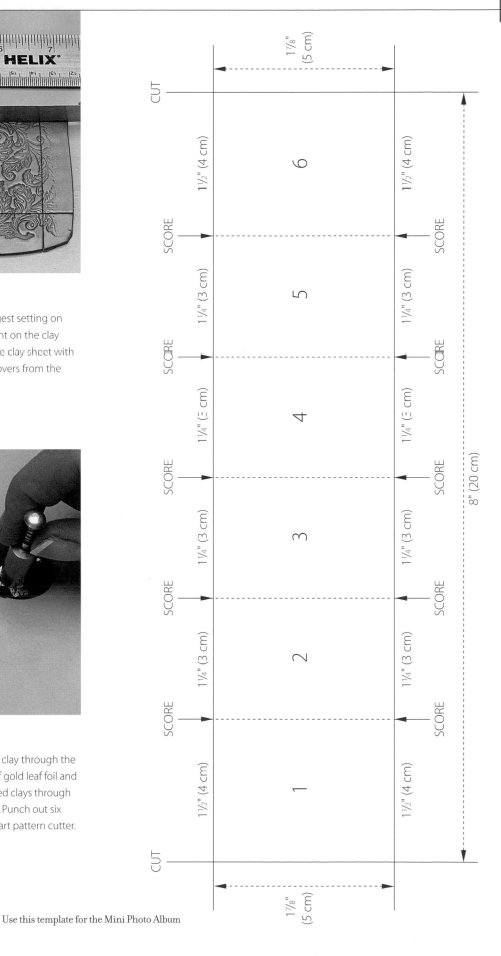

Use this template for the Mini Photo Album

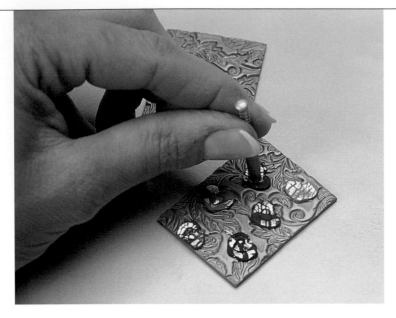

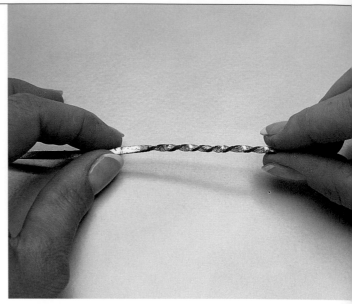

3 Glue the Hearts to the Front Cover
Superglue the hearts onto one of the stamped covers. Impress the center of each heart with the small pattern cutter.

4 Create the Twisted Border
Roll $\frac{1}{8}$ block of purple clay into a 6" (15cm) snake. Roll the snake lengthwise through largest setting of the pasta machine. Apply a piece of gold leaf over the flattened clay. Run this clay lengthwise through the fifth-largest setting of the pasta machine. Cut two 6" x $\frac{1}{8}$" (15cm x 3mm) strips from the foiled purple clay with a clay blade. Twist both strips along their entire length.

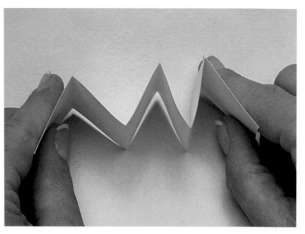

5 Add the Twisted Border to the Book Covers
Superglue the twisted strips around three sides of each cover: two short sides and one long side. Press a knitting needle against the indented sections along the twist to secure. Bake the panels at 270º F (132° C) for twenty-five minutes.

6 Create the Pages of the Photo Album
Cut a $1\frac{7}{8}$" x 8" (5cm x 20cm) strip of white cardstock. Following the lines on the template on page 47, score the cardstock. Fold the cardstock along the score lines, accordion style. You should have five score lines and six panels.

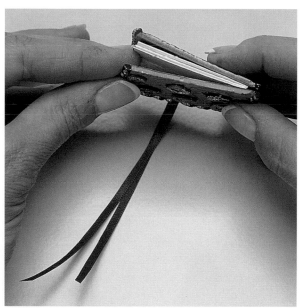

8 Create Back-to-Back Pages

Fold panel 3 onto the exposed adhesive of panel 2. Fold panel 5 onto the exposed adhesive of panel 4.

7 Add the Double-Sided Tape

Cut four squares from a roll of double-sided carpet tape with scissors. Place one square on panels 1, 2, 4, and 6. Remove the tape backing from panels 2 and 4.

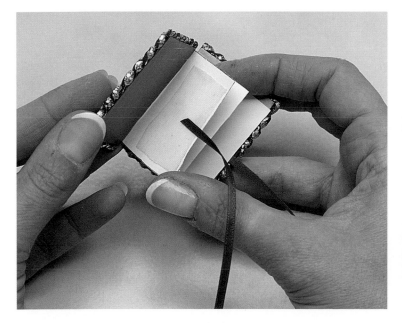

9 Assemble the Book

When the clay panels have cooled, remove the tape backing from panels 1 and 6. Press one 5" (13cm) piece of ribbon halfway over the tape on panel 1 and press another 5" (13cm) piece of ribbon halfway over the tape on panel 6.

10 Add Final Touches

Make sure that the spine of the album is aligned flush with the untrimmed edges of each panel and that the ribbon protrudes from the middle of the long-trimmed edge. If the pages are not properly aligned, the book may not open correctly. Select six photos and trim them to fit inside the album. Attach the photos to each page with a piece of carpet tape.

Keepsake
photo box

If you're like me, you like the idea of scrapbooking, but have little time to devote to detailing page after page. And it would be all but impossible to put all of the thousands of pictures I have into albums or scrapbooks. Whether you're scrapbook-impaired or want an alternative to display your collection of treasured photos, this project is for you. Beaded latticework is embedded into an iridescent polymer clay cover. Leather stamping tools, decoratively cut clay borders, and that very special photo give this project the final touches that turn an economical photo storage box into a beloved keepsake.

materials

- polymer clay

    2 pearl blocks
    1 violet block
    1 white block

- interference violet pearl powder
- flower (PC4F) pattern cutter
- heart (PC3H) pattern cutter
- 2½" (6cm) circle cookie cutter
- small and large flower leather-working stamps
- silver-blue photo box
- blue iridescent triangular glass beads
- 28-gauge black wire

- lavender chenille cord
- epoxy
- superglue
- ball-tip stylus
- carft knife
- eye shadow applicator
- flat paint brush
- metal ruler
- rotary cutter with Victorian edging
- scissors
- wire cutters

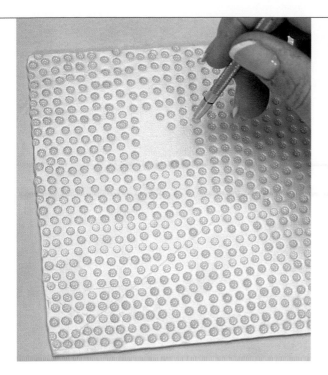

2 Score Diagonal Lines into the Clay

Using the edge of a metal ruler mark diagonal lines from corner to corner of the clay, 1¼" (3cm) apart. Then repeat going in the opposite direction.

1 Create the Box Cover

Roll out two blocks of pearl clay using the largest setting of the pasta machine. Place this sheet on a baking tile. Cut the clay into the dimensions of the box lid. Texture the entire surface with the small flower leather-working stamp.

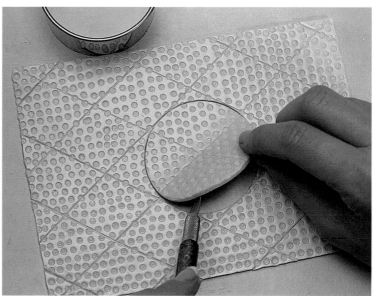

3 Brush on the Violet Pearl Powder

Dip a flat paintbrush into the interference violet powder. Lightly brush the powder onto the clay until the entire surface is covered.

4 Cut Out the Center of the Box

Cut out the center of the clay with a 2½" (6cm) circle cookie cutter. Use the intersecting diagonal lines as a centering guide. Remove the cut clay.

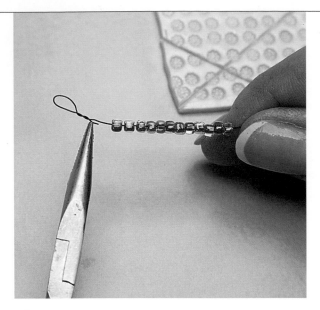

5 String the Beads on Wires

Cut several 10" (25cm) pieces of 28-gauge wire. Bend and twist a small loop into one end of each wire. This will prevent the beads from sliding off. String each wire with 8" (20cm) of beads.

6 Glue the Beading to the Clay

Starting at one corner, brush a 1" (3cm) section of one of the longest diagonal lines with superglue. Starting from the open end of the wire, press the beads onto the glued line. Continue gluing and laying beads, 1" (3cm) at a time, leaving a $^3/_8$" (1cm) gap of exposed wire at each intersecting line.

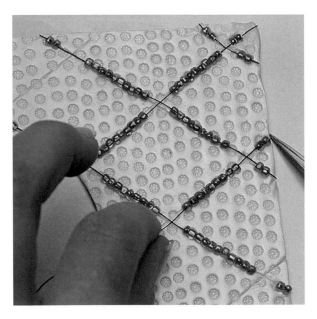

7 Finish the Beaded Lines

To finish off a beaded line, pull the wire loop until the open end extends $^1/_8$" (3mm) over the edge of the clay. Bend the exposed wire end down over the clay and apply a dot of superglue. Slide any unlaid beads at the opposite end to the back of the wire loop. Cut the wire at this end, also leaving a $^1/_8$" (3mm) wire hanging over the edge. Continue until all the lines have been beaded.

8 Punch Out Flowers

Roll $^1/_4$ block of violet clay through the largest setting of the pasta machine. Cut out approximately twenty flowers with the flower cutter. Superglue a flower over each set of exposed intersecting wires.

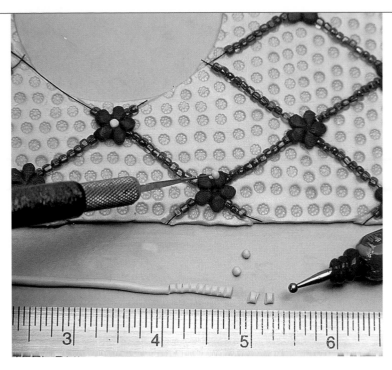

9 Detail the Flowers

Press lines between the petals with the tip of the needle tool. Indent the center of each flower with the large end of the ball-tip stylus. Roll a large ball of white clay into a snake 1/8" (3mm) in diameter. Cut twenty 1/16" (1.5mm) sections and roll them into balls. Press a ball into the center of each flower.

10 Highlight the Flower Petals

Dip a fingertip or eye shadow applicator into interference violet powder and coat each flower. This will highlight the flowers and give the petals a pearlized finish.

11 Add the Heart Border to the Frame

Roll 1/4 block of violet clay through the second-largest setting of the pasta machine. Punch out seventeen hearts with the pattern cutter. Superglue each heart, pointed end out, halfway over the edge of the circle opening in the clay.

12 Detail the Heart Border

Mark three indentions into each heart with the needle tool. Mark a center line straight through the middle of each heart. Mark angled lines on either side of the center line. Bake the beaded clay on the tile at 270° F (132° C) for thirty minutes.

13 Create the Edging for the Box

While the cover is baking, roll ½ block of violet clay into a 17" (43cm) snake. Slightly flatten the snake with your fingers. Run the snake through the pasta machine lengthwise on the third-largest setting. Use a ruler and craft knife to cut a straight edge along one side of the flattened clay snake. Trim the opposite edge to a ⅜" (1cm) width using a rotary cutter.

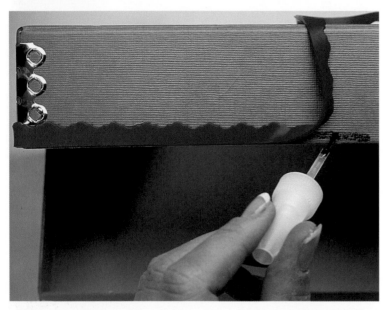

14 Glue the Edging on the Box

Superglue the trimmed strip around the bottom, front and sides of the box lid. Cut the excess clay from the rounded corners with a craft knife.

15 Add Detail to the Edging

Impress each scalloped section of the clay border with the large flower leather-working stamp.

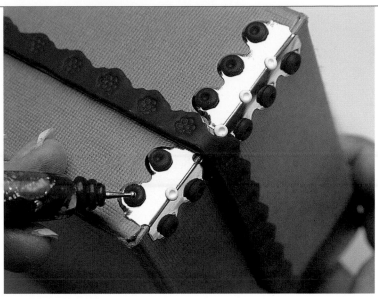

16 Cover the Metal Corners

Roll a ¹⁄₁₆ block of white clay into a snake ¹⁄₈" (3mm) in diameter. Cut sixteen ¹⁄₁₆" (1.5mm) sections with the craft knife. Roll the clay sections into balls and superglue them over the small, center hole openings of each metal corner. Impress them with your stylus.

17 Decorate the Metal Corners

Roll ¹⁄₈ block of violet clay into a snake ¹⁄₈" (3mm) in diameter. Cut the snake into thirty-eight ¹⁄₈" (3mm) sections with the craft knife. Roll the clay sections into balls and superglue them over the large hole openings of the metal corners. Impress the centers with the large end of the stylus. Bake the box at 270° F (132° C), for twenty-five minutes.

18 Add Final Touches

Loosen the cooled lid from the tile by carefully sliding the clay blade under the edges. Center a photo behind the circle opening and tape it in place. Mix a generous amount of the two-part epoxy and spread it over the top of the box. Place the clay panel onto the glued lid. Allow the epoxy to set for five minutes. Super-glue a 28" (71cm) length of chenille cord to the outside edge of the box cover. Cut the excess cord with scissors. If necessary, glue a second row of chenille cord around the lid to hide the wire ends.

polymer clay and desk accessories

Use polymer clay to embellish everyday items found in your office! It is as durable as it is artistic and will make simple office tasks enjoyable.

Techniques such as mica shifting and metal

embossing can make your artistic abilities shine!

Whether you choose to make a checkbook

cover or a business card holder, these projects

will get your creative juices flowing and

personalize any office.

Victorian Business
card holder

t his business card holder is a unique and lovely accessory that you will be proud to carry. You don't carry business cards? Then this case can be a handy repository for your credit cards or wallet-sized photos. Or use it to store the business cards you get from others. Learn the technique for making hand-tinted transfers on polymer clay, and follow these steps to embellish the Victorian image featured on this case with polymer clay flowers and crystals.

materials

- polymer clay
  - 1 green pearl block
  - 1 pearl block
  - 1 purple block
- liquid polymer clay
- flower (PC3F) pattern cutter
- 1½" (4cm) circle cookie cutter
- blank business card holder
- ten 3mm clear flat-back crystals
- colored pencils
- photocopy of copyright-free Victorian image
- acrylic rod or brayer
- clay blade
- craft knife
- epoxy
- ruler
- scissors
- tweezers

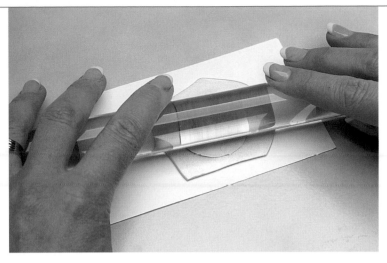

1 Color the Victorian Print

Tint a photocopy of your selected image with colored pencils—you choose the colors! Make sure the picture is sized to fit within a circle 1½" (4cm) in diameter. Color the picture well beyond the 1½" (4cm) area. Place the cookie cutter over the colored print. Lightly trace around the circle and trim the photocopy, cutting slightly beyond the traced circle.

2 Transfer the Print to Clay

Roll ⅛ block of pearl clay through the third largest setting of the pasta machine. Place an index card between the clay sheet and the ceramic tile. Cut a circle in the pearl clay with a 1½" (4cm). Center the tinted photocopy over the clay circle. Burnish the photocopy by rubbing it with your fingers for several seconds and then roll an acrylic brayer over the photocopy two to three times. Bake the clay, with the photocopy on top at 270° F (132° C) for thirty minutes.

3 Create the Case Cover

Lay the card case upside-down over an index card. Trace around the outside edges of the case with a pencil. Use a ruler to draw a smaller rectangle ¼" (6mm) inside the traced pattern. Cut out the smaller rectangle and use it as a template for the case cover. Roll ½ block of green pearl clay through the third-largest setting of the pasta machine. Place the template over the clay sheet and cut around the outside edges with a clay blade. Remove the excess clay.

4 Punch Out the Center and Flowers

Center the clay rectangle over the top of the business card holder. Cut a circle from the center of the green clay with the 1½" (4cm) cookie cutter or template and remove the excess clay. Punch out ten flowers from the green clay with the pattern cutter. Remove the clay flowers with the tip of the craft knife.

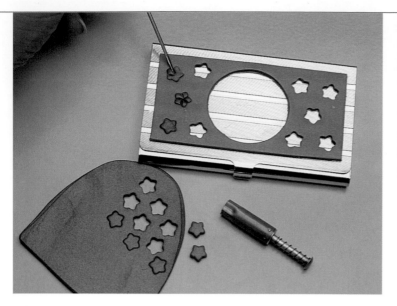

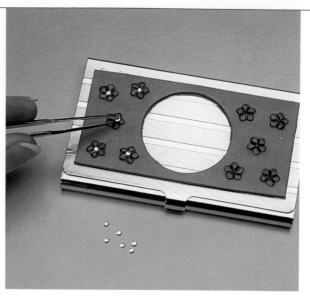

5 Add the Purple Flowers

Blend ¼ block of pearl clay with ⅛ block of purple clay to make lavender pearl clay. Roll a large ball of lavender pearl clay through the second-largest setting of the pasta machine. Punch out ten flowers with the small flower pattern cutter. Press the lavender pearl flowers into the openings in the green pearl clay. Draw in flower petals with the tip of the needle tool.

6 Add Sparkle to Your Flowers

Use tweezers to place a crystal over the center of each flower. Press the crystals into the clay using the tweezer handle.

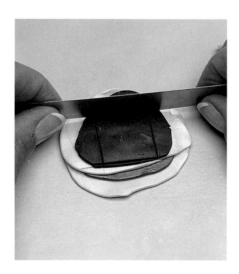

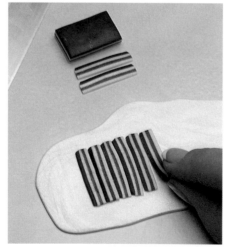

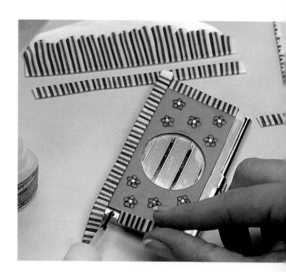

7 Begin the Striped Design

Roll two large balls of pearl clay, one large ball of lavender pearl clay and one large ball of purple clay through the third-largest setting of the pasta machine. Stack these clays over each other in the following order: pearl, lavender pearl, pearl, and purple. Cut this stack into a 1" x 1" (3cm x 3cm) square with the clay blade.

8 Line Up the Stripes

Roll ¹⁄₁₆ block of pearl clay into a 4" (10cm) snake. Run this snake through the fourth-largest setting of the pasta machine. Slice ten ¹⁄₁₆" (1.5mm) thick slices from the striped clay stack. Lay each slice side by side on the pearl clay sheet, alternating colors. Roll the striped sheet (stripes facing up) through the third-largest setting of the pasta machine.

9 Create the Striped Border

Cut four strips ¼" (6mm) wide from the striped clay sheet. Superglue the strips around the edge of the case to create the border. Trim off any excess. Bake the case at 270° F (132° C) for thirty minutes. Allow the case to cool.

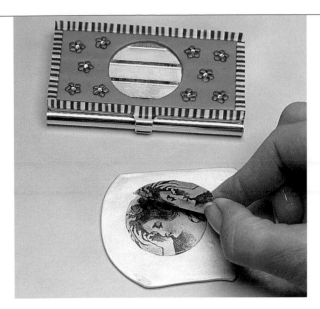

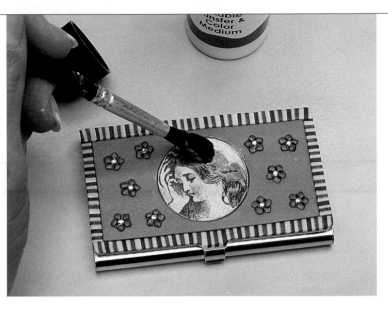

10 Add the Victorian Print

Peel the print off the cooled pearl clay. Remove the trimmed image from the baked pearl sheet. Superglue the image transfer into the center of the baked card case.

11 Reinforce With Liquid Polymer Clay

Brush a very thin layer of liquid polymer clay over the surface of the image transfer. Be sure to work the liquid polymer clay into the crevice between the green pearl clay and the image transfer. Wipe away any excess liquid polymer clay from the green pearl clay.

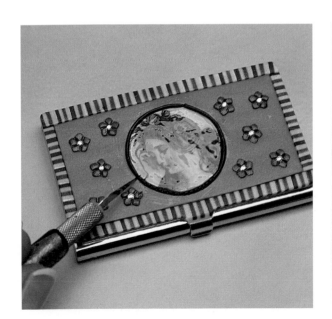

12 Frame the Victorian Print

Roll a small ball of purple clay into a snake 1/16" (1.5mm) in diameter. Press the snake down around the crevice outside the image. With the dull edge of a craft knife, make lines every 1/16" (1.5mm) around the purple clay border. The clay stretches as the marks are made, so trim any excess purple clay after the last mark has been made. Bake the case again at 270° F (132° C) for thirty minutes.

13 Add Final Touches

When the case is cool, carefully slide the clay blade under the edges to loosen the clay from the case. Mix the two-part epoxy and apply a thin layer to the cover of the case. Place the clay cover over the glued surface of the card case. Press the clay down firmly to remove any air pockets. Let the epoxy set a full twenty-four hours before using the case.

Mesh Pencil
caddy

l ooking for a stylish way to hold all those pens and pencils? In this project, wire mesh and clay are combined to make a contemporary accessory that will lend style to any desk. Learn how to use an armature to support a three-dimensional form. Pattern cutters and boldly colored clay are used to create a simple but stunning symmetry with this layered design.

materials

- polymer clay

  1 gold block
  1 black block
  2 pearl blocks

- liquid polymer clay

- small (PC1SQ), medium (PCBSQ) and large (PCASQ) square pattern cutters

- small (PC2T) teardrop pattern cutter

- 3" (8cm) circle cookie cutter

- wire mesh

- cloth measuring tape

- 16-ounce (473ml) empty water bottle

- superglue

- clay blade

- clay shaper

- ruler

- stapler

- tape

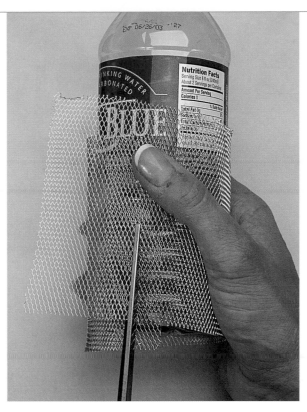

1 Create the Base of the Pencil Caddy

Roll ½ block of black clay through the largest setting of the pasta machine and fold it in half. Cut out a 3" (8cm) circle from the doubled clay with the cookie cutter.

2 Measure the Wire Mesh

Cut a piece of wire mesh 4" x 10" (10cm x 25cm) and wrap it around the water bottle. Trim the wire mesh with scissors, leaving a ½" (1cm) overlap around the width of the bottle.

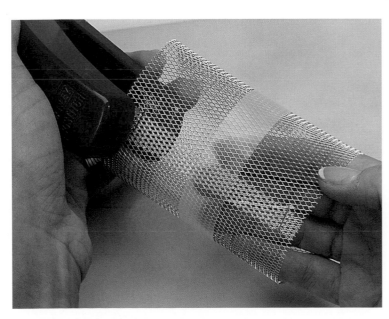

3 Reinforce the Wire Mesh

Apply a strip of tape along the middle of the wire mesh around the entire bottle. Carefully slide the taped form off the bottle. Staple the seams of the wire mesh together at the top and bottom. Remove the tape and staple the seam at the center. Place the mesh circle back over the bottle.

4 Connect the Base

Center the bottle with wire mesh over the black clay circle. Gently press the bottom ⅛" (3mm) of the wire mesh into the clay base of the pencil caddy. Brush liquid polymer clay around the base where the wire mesh and clay meet. Bake the base at 270° F (132° C), for forty minutes.

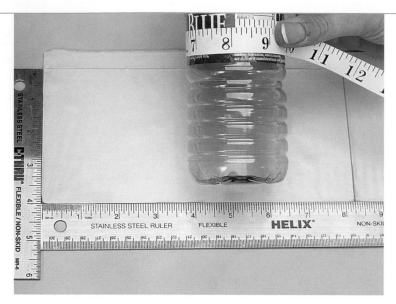

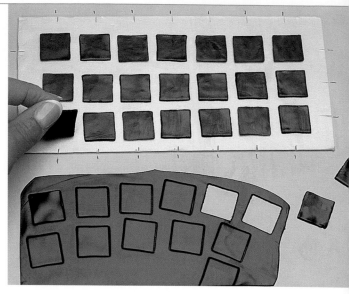

5 Roll Out the Pearl Clay

Measure the circumference of the bottle with the cloth measuring tape. Combine the two blocks of pearl clay and roll through the second-largest setting of the pasta machine. Trim the clay sheet so that it measures 4" (10cm) wide. To determine the length of the clay, take the bottle circumference and add ³⁄₈" (1cm). Trim the clay sheet's length to this measurement.

6 Begin the Pencil Caddy Design

Use a ruler to mark seven evenly spaced segments along the bottom of the pearl clay. Roll ¹⁄₂ block of black clay through the fourth-largest setting of the pasta machine. Punch out twenty-four ³⁄₄" (2cm) black clay squares with the largest pattern cutter. Place three black clay squares over each measured mark, spacing them evenly to form three rows.

7 Add the Gold Squares

Roll ¹⁄₂ block of gold clay through the fourth-largest setting of the pasta machine. Punch out twenty-four gold clay squares with the medium square pattern cutter. Place a gold square over each of the twenty-one black squares. Note: You will have three left-over black squares and three left-over gold squares.

8 Punch Out the Squares

Cut out the center of each layered clay square with the small square pattern cutter.

9 Trim the Excess

With a clay blade, trim approximately ¹⁄₈" (3mm) away from the marked edge of the clay sheet. Carefully loosen the clay sheet from the work surface with the clay blade.

10 Wrap the Clay Around the Armature

Place the water bottle back into the cooled wire mesh form for added support. Wrap the pearl clay sheet around the wire mesh form. Trim any overlapping clay. Blend the clay seam together with your fingertip or a clay shaper.

11 Add Another Row of Squares

Press the three remaining gold squares over the center of the three remaining black clay squares. Center the layered squares over the blended seam on the pearl clay, matching the spacing of the previously applied squares. Cut out the center of the three squares with a small square pattern cutter. Remove the water bottle. Cut off any wire extending beyond the top of the clay sheet with scissors.

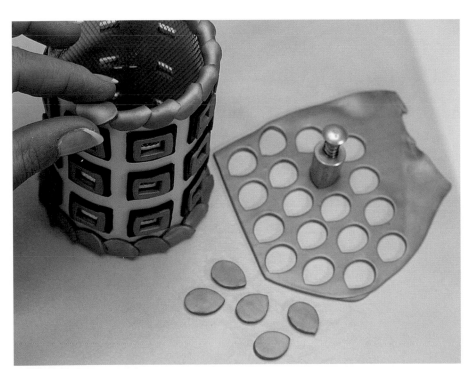

12 Add Final Touches

Roll ½ block of gold clay through the second-largest setting of the pasta machine. Cut out forty teardrop shapes with the small pattern cutter. Superglue the teardrops, scallop fashion, over the top and bottom edges of the wire mesh and clay. Bend the edges down slightly with your fingers. Bake at 270° F (132° C) for forty-five minutes.

Fower Pen &
stand

t ired of never having a pen within reach? Here's
a pen with a holder so unique, it's bound to stick
around. Fun and practical at the same time, this
whimsical millefiori pen begs to be put back where it
belongs. With its combination of wire and clay, this
refillable pen can be used for years to come!

materials

- polymer clay
  - 1 black block
  - 1 turquoise pearl block
  - 2 purple blocks
  - 2 white blocks

- ballpoint pen (I used a BicStick
  pen because they won't melt)

- ten 3mm clear flat-back crystals

- one 5mm flat-back crystal

- 34" (86cm) purple plastic-
  coated 18-gauge wire

- epoxy

- superglue

- lipstick tube, ¾" (2cm) in
  diameter

- ball-tip stylus

- needle-nose pliers

- wire cutters

- toothpicks

- tweezers

- knitting needle (optional)

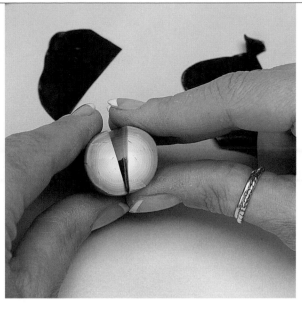

1 Slice a Skinner Blend Cane in Half

Make a white and turquoise Skinner Blend cane following the directions on pages 14–15. Cut 1½" (4cm) from the cane and stand it on its end. Cut the cane in half. Roll a large ball of black clay through the fifth-largest setting of the pasta machine. Cut a straight edge along one side of the black clay with a clay blade. Lay one piece of the cane halfway over the straight edge of the black clay sheet. Trim the excess black clay away from the bottom and sides of the half cane.

2 Wrap the Combined Halves

Press the two halves of the cut cane (with the black strip sandwiched in between) back together. Roll ¼ block of black clay through the fourth-largest setting of the pasta machine. Wrap this clay around the entire cane. Trim off the excess clay.

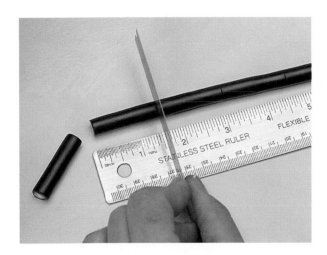

3 Lengthen the Cane

Cut a ½" (1cm) piece from this cane and set it aside until step 13. Roll and reduce the remaining cane to 9" (23cm) long. Trim off the distorted ends and cut five 1½" (4cm) sections from the 9" (23cm) cane.

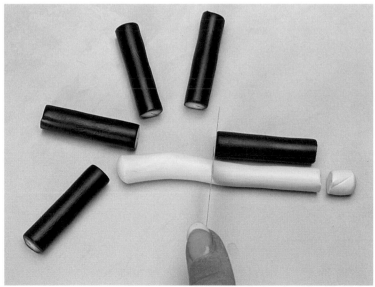

4 Make a White Snake

Roll ¼ block of white clay into a snake the same diameter as the five cane sections. Cut the white snake to 1½" (4cm) long. Wrap the white snake in black clay that has been rolled through the fourth-largest setting of the pasta machine. Save the excess for step 13.

Rolling a cane back and forth under the blade while slicing will help prevent distortion of the cane shape.

TIP

5 Create the Flower Cane

Place the five cane sections around the wrapped white center to form the flower. The center vein in each petal should be pointing outward from the white center. Check both sides of the flower cane to be sure that the petals are properly aligned.

6 Make a Lavender Triangular Snake

Blend one block of white and ¼ block of purple to make lavender clay. Roll a 1" (3cm) ball of lavender clay into a snake ¼" (6mm) in diameter. Pinch the top of the snake along the length between your thumb and index finger to form a triangle.

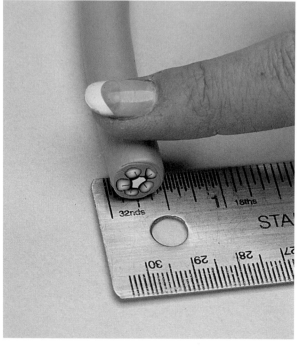

7 Place the Lavender Clay Between the Petals

Cut the lavender snake into five 1½" (4cm) sections. Tightly pack the lavender clay into the flower cane by pressing down on each section with the handle of your needle tool. Roll the remaining lavender clay through the third-largest setting of the pasta machine. Wrap the flower cane in the lavender clay.

8 Reduce the Diameter of the Flower Cane

Cut a 1" (3cm) section of the flower cane. Reduce the cane to ⅜" (1cm) in diameter. Allow the cane to rest or freeze for fifteen minutes before using.

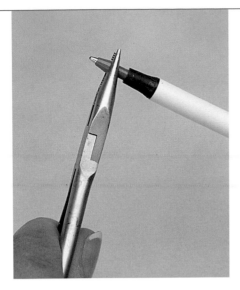

9 Prepare the Pen

Carefully remove the ink cartridge from the pen by twisting and then pulling with the needle-nose pliers. Set the ink cartridge aside.

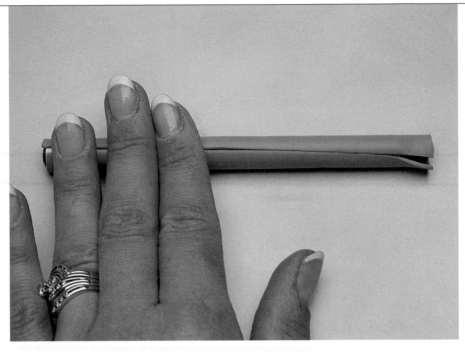

10 Cover the Pen Barrel with Lavender Clay

Roll the remaining lavender clay into a 5" (13cm) snake. Run the snake through the pasta machine on the third-largest setting. Wrap the pen barrel in the lavender clay sheet. Trim the excess clay from the top and bottom of the pen. Roll the clay-covered barrel against your work surface with the palm of your hand to blend the seam together.

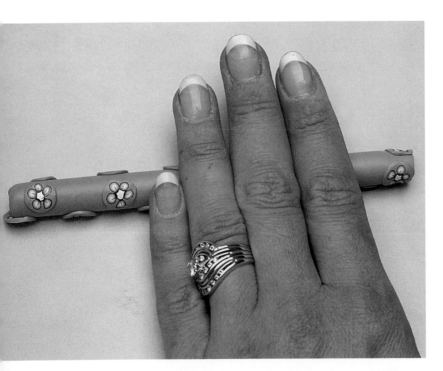

11 Add the Cane Slices

Slice several dozen ¹⁄₁₆" (1.5mm) thick slices from the reduced flower cane. Lay the slices randomly over the lavender clay-covered pen barrel. Roll the pen against your work surface again until the cane slices blend into the lavender clay base. Trim the excess clay from the top and bottom of the pen barrel with a craft knife.

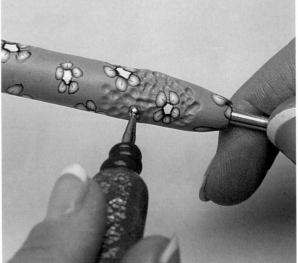

12 Stipple the Pen Barrel

Stipple the surface of the lavender clay with the small end of a ball-tip stylus. Tip: The pen will be easier to handle while texturing if placed on a knitting needle.

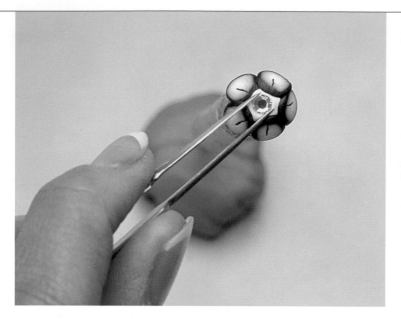

13 Add a Flower to the Top of the Pen

Smooth the clay at the top of the pen and superglue a flattened ball of white clay to it. Reduce the left-over petal cane from step 4, to ³⁄₈" (1cm) in diameter. Slice five thin slices from the cane and superglue around the outer edge of the white clay ball to make a flower. The center veins should be facing outward from the white center. Press a 5mm crystal into the white clay using the handle of the tweezers. Bake the pen on an index card at 270º F (132° C), for thirty minutes. Optional: Polish the pen when cool. (see page 13 for polishing instructions).

14 Create the Base of the Pen Stand

Roll two 1¹⁄₂" (4cm) balls of purple clay and one 1" (3cm) ball of lavender clay. Slightly flatten each ball by pressing with the palm of your hand against the work surface. Insert two toothpicks directly opposite one another halfway into the lavender clay ball. Press the purple clay balls onto the exposed ends of the toothpicks, connecting all three balls.

15 Add Dots to the Lavender Ball

Roll a small ball of black clay into a snake ¹⁄₈" (3mm) in diameter. Cut about twenty ¹⁄₈" (3mm) sections from the snake. Roll them into tiny balls. Press the balls randomly over the surface of the lavender ball. Flatten these balls with your fingertip.

16 Finish Detailling the Lavender Ball

Roll a tiny ball of white clay into a snake ¹⁄₁₆" (1.5mm) in diameter. Cut twenty ¹⁄₁₆" (1.5mm) sections. Roll these sections into balls. Press the white balls over the flattened black clay balls. Press the small end of the ball-tip stylus into the center of each white ball.

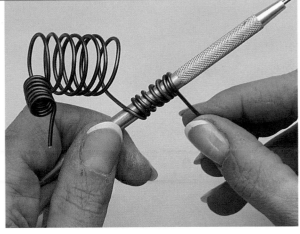

17 Add Flowers to the Purple Balls

Roll two ³/₈" (1cm) balls of white clay. Press each ball over the top-center of each purple clay ball. Slightly flatten these with your finger. Cut ten ¹/₈" (3mm) slices from the large petal cane section set aside in step 3. Place five cane slices around each of the white balls on the purple clay. The center veins should be pointing outward.

18 Coil the Wire for the Stand

Bend ¹/₂" (1cm) at one end of the 36" (91cm) purple coated wire at a 90° angle to form a tail. Starting right after the tail, wrap the wire around the handle of the needle tool seven times. Remove the needle tool and wrap the next section of wire around a ³/₄" (2cm) diameter lipstick tube six times. Wrap the remaining wire around the needle tool handle seven more times. Remove the needle tool. Trim any remaining wire to ¹/₂" (1cm) with the wire cutters. Bend the last ¹/₂" (1cm) of wire to form another tail.

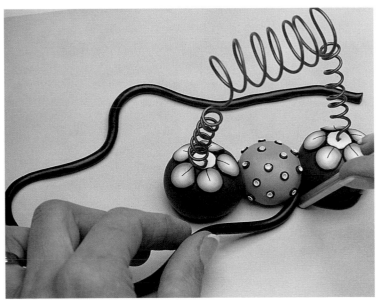

19 Insert the Wire Into the Stand

Bend the tails on both wire ends so that they face downward from the small coils. Insert a tail into the center of each flower on the stand. The wire may sit crookedly. You can adjust it after baking.

20 Add Final Touches

Roll ¹/₄ block of black clay into a snake ¹/₄" (6mm) in diameter. Wrap the snake around the base of the stand. Cut off the excess clay. Blend the seam in the border together with your fingertip. Bake at 270° F (132° C) for one hour. When the stand is completely cool, carefully pull the wire out. Mix epoxy and insert it into the holes with a toothpick. Insert the coiled wire into the glued holes. Let the glue set fifteen to twenty minutes. Bend the wire to adjust if needed.

Mica Checkbook
cover

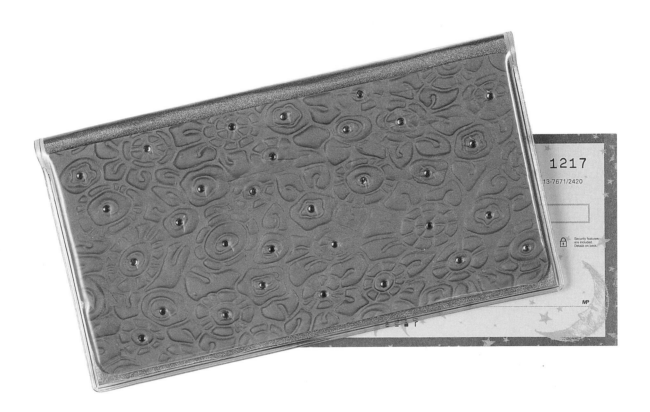

You'll look like a million bucks, carrying this elegant checkbook cover. The amazing mica shift technique leaves a holographic-type design embedded in the clay. Learn the rubber stamp technique for creating a look that appears textured, but is completely smooth. Crystals add the finishing touch, guaranteed to get oohs and aahs— even if your bank balance is less than stunning.

materials

- polymer clay
  - 1 metallic gold block (no glitter)
- flower rubber stamp
- clear checkbook cover
- thirty 3mm topaz flat-back crystals
- acrylic floor wax
- automotive protectant
- 1 piece thin cardboard
- epoxy

- 600-grit, 800-grit and 1000-grit automotive grade wet-dry sandpaper
- acrylic rod or brayer
- clay blade
- paintbrush
- scissors
- buffer (optional)
- soft cotton cloth (optional)

1 Stamp the Gold Clay

Roll one block of conditioned gold clay through the largest setting of the pasta machine six or seven times. Roll the sheet to approximately 3" x 6" (8cm x 15cm). Spray automotive protectant on the clay and spread it with your fingers. Place the sprayed clay, face down, over the rubber stamp. Starting at one side of the stamp, firmly roll an acrylic brayer across the clay. Make only one pass (repeated passes will leave shadow impressions in the clay).

2 Shave the Stamped Impression

Working with a very sharp clay blade on small sections at a time, shave off only the raised portions of the clay. Be careful not to cut too deeply! Continue this process until the entire stamped surface is flat. Shaving the raised areas will leave a "ghost" image of the pattern embedded in the clay. Save your shavings!

3 Repair Any Areas Cut Too Deeply

If you have found that you have cut too deeply, turn over some of the saved shavings with the craft knife. Place shavings over any areas that have no visible pattern because they were cut too deeply. Don't get discouraged. While this technique is simple in concept, it takes a little practice to perfect.

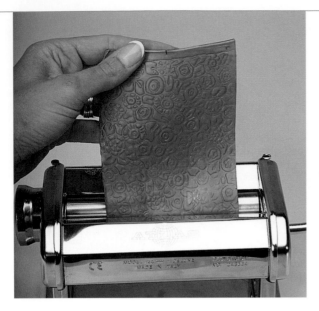

4 Smooth Out the Clay

Spray automotive protectant onto an acrylic brayer or rod, and spread with your fingers. Roll the shaved clay sheet with the brayer until it is smooth and even. Run the smoothed sheet through the third-largest setting of the pasta machine.

5 Create the Template

Draw a 2⅞" x 5⅞" (7cm x 15cm) rectangle onto a thin sheet of cardboard. Cut out the rectangle. Round the two bottom corners with a pair of scissors. Place the template over the clay sheet and cut around the edges with the clay blade. Remove any excess clay.

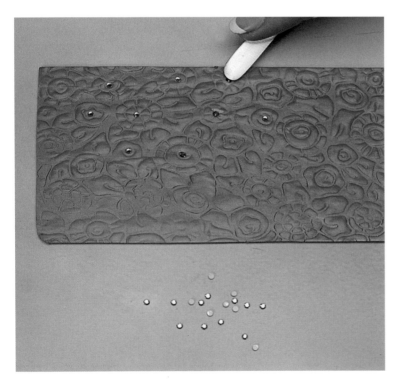

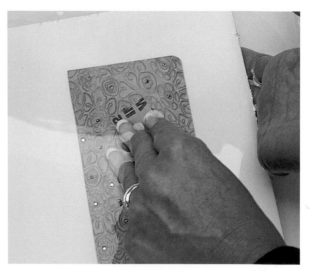

7 Sand the Clay

When the clay is completely cool and still attached to the baking tile, sand it in a sink filled with water. Start with 600-grit, wet-dry sandpaper. Repeat sanding with pieces of 800-grit and 1000-grit paper. Rinse the clay and dry it with a cotton cloth.

6 Add Crystals to the Clay

Place crystals onto the centers of most of the flowers with tweezers. Press them into the clay with the tweezer handle. Bake the clay on the work tile at 270° F (132° C) for thirty minutes.

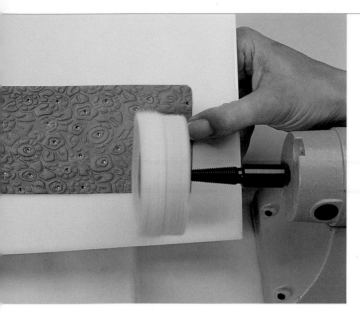

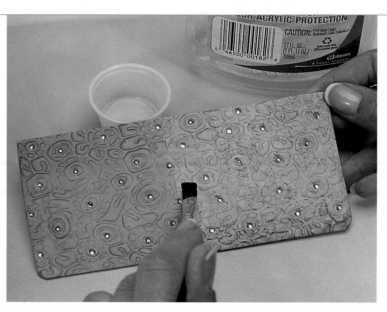

8 Polish and Buff the Clay

The clay can be hand-buffed by vigorously polishing with a piece of old denim or 100% cotton cloth. This will give the clay a satin finish that may be glazed for added shine. For a glasslike finish, hold the clay against the tile and buff on a muslin polishing wheel. (For more information on a polishing wheel see page 13).

9 Add a Glaze Finish

Brush a light coat of acrylic floor wax on the clay. Let it dry for fifteen to twenty minutes.

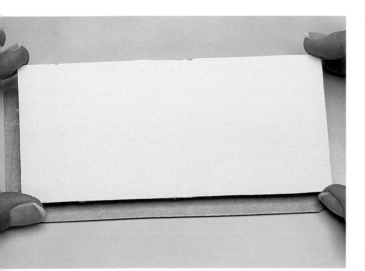

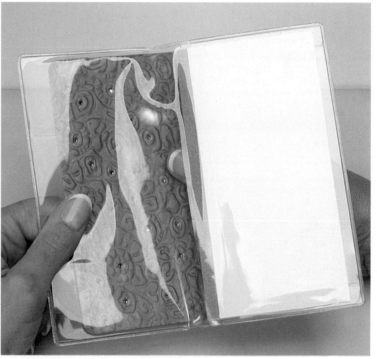

10 Trim the Cardboard

Cut off a 1/8" (3mm) strip along one width and one length of the cardboard template. This compensates for the small amount of clay shrinkage that occurs while baking. Re-round the two bottom corners with scissors. Mix epoxy and spread it on the back of the cardboard template.

11 Add Final Touches

Place the glued cardboard template over the back of the clay insert. Roll the backing with the brayer to force out trapped air. Let the glue set for fifteen minutes. Slip the clay into a clear checkbook cover.

polymer clay and jewelry

Wearing the products of your efforts or seeing them worn by a friend is the most rewarding result of your creativity.

Jewelry has long been one of the most widely used forms of adornment and self-expression. These days, anything goes, from art deco to ethnic. Whether you are trying to match your dress or your mood, jewelry becomes a fabulous extension of your personality. Polymer clay is an ideal medium for jewelry crafting. In these projects, you can learn techniques to make wearable, personal ornaments you will be happy to wear or give with pride.

Heart Locket
pin

t his delightful brooch is a touching way to display your love. A hinged clay cover lifts to reveal one or two photos of your loved ones. Rubber-stamp embossing and Skinner Blend leaves give this locket a striking look that's bound to get attention.

materials

- polymer clay
  - 1 red block
  - 1 pearl block
  - 1 white block
- liquid polymer clay
- white pearlized powder
- Victorian heart stamp
- black rubber stamp pad
- ³⁄₄" (2cm) silver pin backing
- silver eye pin
- small brass hinge

- sterling silver heart charm with jump ring
- small photograph
- double-sided adhesive
- epoxy
- superglue
- clay blade
- needle-nose pliers
- needle tool
- wire cutters

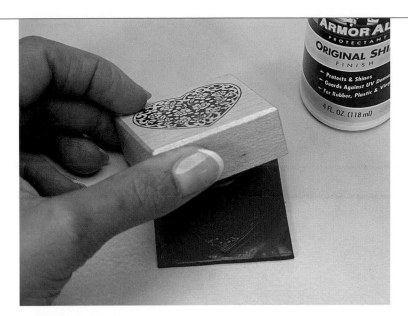

1 Stamp the Heart on Red Clay

Roll out ¼ block of red clay on the third-largest setting of the pasta machine. Spray the clay with automotive protectant and spread it with your fingers. Impress the clay deeply with the rubber stamp, leaving a raised pattern.

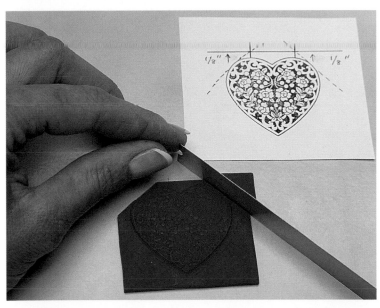

2 Create a Heart Template

Ink the stamp and press it onto an index card. Measure and mark a distance of ⅛" (3mm) over the center-top of each hump on the stamped heart. Use a ruler to draw a straight horizontal line connecting these two marks. Using the ruler again, draw diagonal lines, connecting the top of each ⅛" (3mm) mark to the upper right and left sides of the heart, as shown. Cut out the heart with scissors and use it as a template to cut out the locket cover.

3 Antique the Heart

Brush the raised areas of the heart with pearlized powder. Add more powder as needed until all of the raised areas of stamped clay are antiqued.

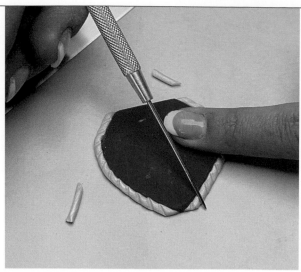

4 Add the Cane Border

Make a white and red Skinner Blend cane (see instructions on page 14). Cut a 1/2" (1cm) section from the cane. Roll and reduce this section to 3/8" (1cm) in diameter. Pinch along the length of the cane between your thumb and index finger to form a teardrop shape. Let the cane rest or freeze for fifteen minutes. Cut seventeen 1/16" (1.5mm) thick slices with the clay blade. Flip the cane back and forth between each slice to prevent distorting the cane's shape. Starting at the bottom, superglue the slices in scallop fashion outlining the heart.

5 Create the Heart Backing and Border

Roll the excess red clay through the fourth-largest setting of the pasta machine. Use the index card template to cut out back of the locket. Cut around the outside of the heart. Roll 1/8 block of pearl clay into a snake 3/16" (5mm) in diameter. Cut two 2 1/2" (6cm) pieces from the snake. Superglue each section to the outside edges of heart and trim any excess clay. Impress diagonal lines every 1/8" (3mm) with the tip of the needle tool.

6 Insert the Eye Pin

Cut a silver eye pin to 1/2" (1cm) in length with the wire cutters. Insert the eye pin into the bottom of the pin backing.

7 Add the Hinge

Place the stamped heart face-down on an index card on the work tile. Set the backing (face-up) on a stack of index cards high enough to set the back heart level with the stamped heart. Determine the direction that the hinge opens and closes before gluing. Place the two hearts directly opposite one another, with a 1/8" (3mm) gap between them. Superglue the opened hinge onto each heart. Lightly press both sides of the hinge into the clay with the tip of the craft knife.

Use superglue sparingly! Too much will ruin the moving mechanism of the hinge.
TIP

8 Add Clay to Hide the Hinge

Brush a thin coat of liquid polymer clay over each side of the hinge end and onto the red clay. Be careful to not get liquid polymer into the hinge mechanism. Roll a small ball of red clay through the sixth-largest setting of the pasta machine. Cut two rectangles, slightly larger than each hinge half, from the red clay sheet. Place each rectangle over the liquid polymer-coated hinges. Blend the edges of the clay rectangles onto the clay of the hearts with your fingertip or a clay shaper. Without disturbing the hearts (the locket back should still be sitting on the stack of index cards) bake the hearts on the work tile at 270° F (132° C) for thirty-five minutes.

9 Add the Photo

Trim the heart template to remove the guide marks so that only the stamped portion remains. Use this as a cutting guide for your photo. Cut out a picture and attach it to the inside of the cooled hinged heart with double-sided adhesive.

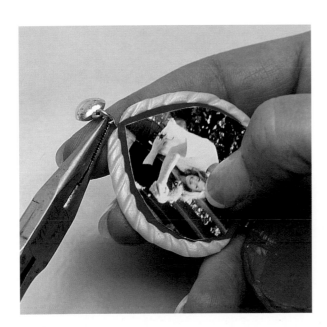

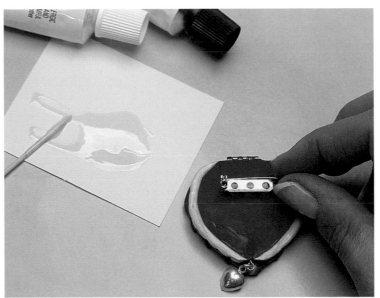

10 Attach the Heart Charm

Use needle-nose pliers to open the jump ring attached to the heart charm. Place the open jump ring through the eye pin and close it with the pliers.

11 Add the Pin Backing

Mix two-part epoxy and glue the pin backing to the back of the heart. Allow to the glue to set for twenty-four hours before wearing.

Spirit Song
amulet

t *his tiny vessel opens to reveal an enclosed wish or prayer. Any sentiment can be written on a tiny piece of parchment and enclosed within. A heart-shaped opening frames your, symbol or initials. This is an ideal present for a loved one who travels, someone in need of healing, or just to say you care. You can even make one for yourself!*

materials

- polymer clay
  - 1 blue pearl block
  - 1 gold block
  - 1 pearl block
- small (PC2H) heart pattern cutter
- 2 blue glass accent beads
- silver bullet-style earring backing
- 3" (8cm) twisted silver eye pin
- silver jump ring
- silver chain (any length and style)
- ballpoint pen
- black, fine-tip permanent marker
- parchment paper
- clay blade
- needle-nose pliers
- wire cutters
- tweezers

1 Stack the Clay

Roll ⅛ block each of pearl, blue pearl, and gold clays through the third-largest setting of the pasta machine. Stack the clays from lightest to darkest and trim to a 1" x 1" (3cm x 3cm) square with the clay blade. Roll the trimmed, stacked clay through the third-largest setting of the pasta machine.

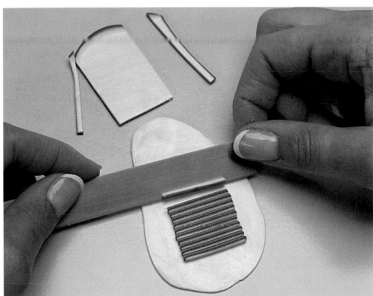

2 Create a Striped Sheet

Roll ⅛ block of pearl clay through the fourth-largest setting of the pasta machine. Cut ten ⅛" (3mm) thick slices from this stack and lay them side by side (alternating colors), over the pearl clay sheet. Run this sheet through the third-largest setting of the pasta machine to make a striped clay sheet.

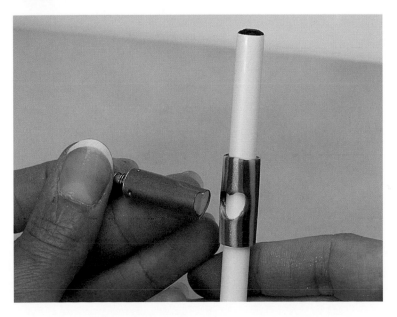

3 Make the Amulet

Trim the edges of the flattened, striped sheet to 1" (3cm) wide. Cut a straight edge on one end of the clay strip. Remove the ink cartridge from a ballpoint pen with needle-nose pliers and use the barrel as an armature. Starting at the straight edge, wrap the striped sheet around the pen barrel. Cut off the excess clay and smooth out the seam. Cut a heart-shaped opening from the center of the amulet body with the small pattern cutter. Bake the amulet and the pen barrel on a ceramic tile at 270° F (132° C) for twenty-five minutes. When the clay has cooled, twist the clay to loosen it from the pen barrel.

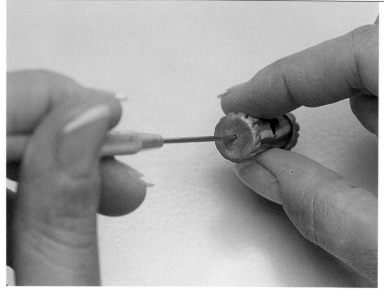

4 Add the Amulet Caps

Roll two ⁷⁄₁₆" (4mm) balls of gold clay. Slightly flatten the balls between your thumb and index finger. Press a ball onto each end of the amulet body.

5 Add Detail to the Amulet Caps

Mark diagonal lines into the edge of the gold caps with the tip of the needle tool. Make a hole in the top and bottom of the gold caps using the needle tool. Stand the amulet on the work tile and bake it again at 270° F (132° C) for twenty-five minutes.

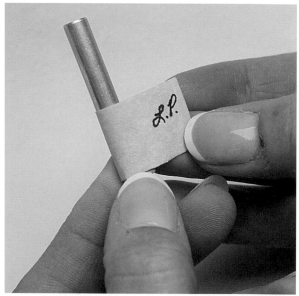

6 Create the Parchment Message

When the amulet has cooled, gently pry off the top and bottom caps. Hand write or print a short prayer, poem or sentiment on a 1½" x 1¼" (4cm x 3cm) piece of parchment.

7 Roll the Parchment Insert

Near the top-right corner on the back of the parchment, draw a tiny symbol or initials with the permanent marker. Fold the parchment in half. Roll the folded paper around the handle of the needle tool.

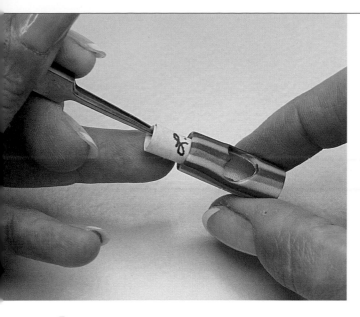

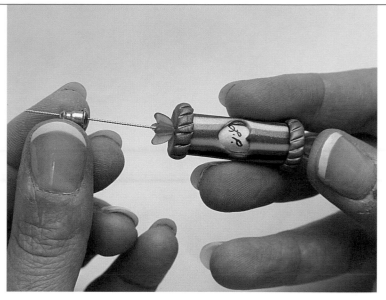

8 Insert the Parchment into the Amulet

Slide the rolled parchment off the handle and insert it into the amulet with tweezers. Turn the parchment so that the drawn symbol shows through the heart opening.

9 Assemble the Amulet

Press the top clay cap on the amulet. Thread a blue accent bead onto the eye pin. Push the eye pin into the hole of the clay cap and down through the amulet body. Thread the bottom gold cap over the exposed eye pin and onto the amulet body. Thread another blue accent bead onto the eye pin. Push the earring backing onto the exposed eye pin to hold it in place.

10 Add Final Details

Cut any excess length from the eye pin with wire cutters. Attach a chain to the eye pin using needle-nose pliers. Open the eye pin loop by grasping the looped end with needle-nose pliers and swinging the loop out. (Do not pull the loop back away from eye pin, as this will distort the shape of the loop.) Insert a jump ring attached to a chain into the open end of the eye pin. Swing the open end of the eye pin loop back into place with pliers. Now the amulet is ready to wear or give proudly!

Heart
pendant

f *abric foils aren't just for fabric. I found a way to re-create the look of costly dichroic glass using these mylar-backed foils. The technique is used to create a heart-shaped pendant that could pass for a dichroic glass bead. Learn the secret to making polymer clay imitate the colorful iridescence of this spectacular glass medium.*

materials

- polymer clay
  - 1 black block
- liquid polymer clay
- fabric foil, assorted colors
- 30" (76cm) rubber cording
- 600-grit, 800-grit and 1000-grit wet-dry sandpaper
- acrylic floor wax

- black, fine-tip permanent marker
- clay shaper
- clay tool
- assorted knitting needles
- buffer (optional)
- soft cloth (optional)
- diluent (optional)

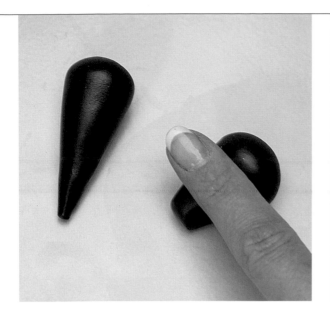

1 Make the Heart

Roll 2 ¼ blocks of black clay into 2" (5cm) long teardrop shapes. Press the teardrop shapes together to form a heart. Slightly flatten the heart against the work surface with the palm of your hand.

2 Fill in the Heart

Roll a small ball of black clay into a snake ⅛" (3mm) in diameter. Starting at the top of the heart, lay the snake along the center of the heart, filling in the center crevice. Trim any excess clay from the bottom of the heart. Blend the clay snake into the heart with your fingertips or a clay shaper.

3 Add the Fabric Foil

Roll ¼ block of black clay through the fourth-largest setting of the pasta machine. Cut small fabric foil squares in assorted colors. Warm a piece of foil between the palms of your hands for one minute. Lay the warmed foil on the clay. Burnish a small spot on the foil square by rubbing back and forth with your index finger. Quickly pull the foil from the clay. Repeat this step with the remaining foil squares, until most of the clay's surface is covered with splashes of metallic color.

4 Cover the Heart with Foiled Clay

Slide the clay blade under the foiled sheet and lift it from the work surface. Place the sheet over the clay heart and smooth the top surface with your fingers.

5 Wrap Foil Around the Back of the Heart

Turn the foil-covered heart over on your work surface. Trim the foiled clay sheet, leaving an excess ¼" (6mm) border all around the heart. Cut darts into the foiled clay sheet along the border. Wrap these darts around the sides and back of the heart.

6 Smooth Out the Heart

Smooth clay on the sides of the heart with a clay shaper or your fingers. Impress the crevice at the top-center of the heart with the tip of a knitting needle or clay tool.

7 Add the Heart Backing

Roll ⅛ block of black clay through the fifth-largest setting of the pasta machine. Cut a heart, slightly smaller than the foiled heart, from the black clay. Place the black clay heart on the back of the foiled heart. Smooth it with a clay shaper or your index finger to create a finished look on the back.

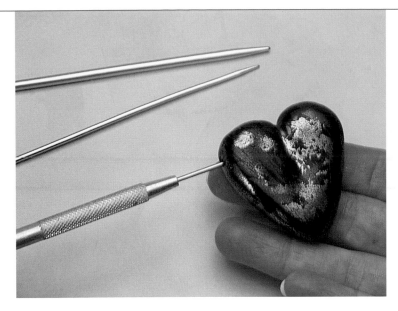

8 Push a Hole Through the Heart

Push the needle tool all the way through the top portion of the heart as shown. Be careful not to place the hole too high. Twist the needle tool a few times to enlarge the hole, then remove. Repeat this step with a small, medium and large knitting needle to expand the hole size. Leave the largest knitting needle in the heart. Note: These instructions are for making a hole large enough for the cording, however you may create a smaller hole if you would like to use a chain.

9 Seal the Heart

Leaving the largest knitting needle in place, brush the top and sides of the heart with a very thin coat of liquid polymer clay. Note: You may want to thin the liquid polymer clay with diluent before using as it is rather thick. Bake at 270° F (132° C) for forty minutes. When the heart has cooled, twist the knitting needle back and forth to loosen and pull it from the heart.

10 Add Final Touches

When the heart has cooled, you may want to sand, polish and glaze the heart following the directions on page 13. An unpolished heart is shown at left; the heart on the right has been polished. String the rubber cording through the hole in the heart. Trim the cord to the desired hanging length and tie off the ends or add a jewelry clasp and wear!

polymer clay and home décor

Your home is the ideal place to express yourself.

Few places in our lives offer the freedom to convey our life interests and sense of personal style as well as our homes. What better satisfaction than to see the fruits of your creative efforts as you walk from room to room? Showcase your creativity both inside and out! Polymer clay can enhance and embellish objects that vary from traditional to contemporary. By employing rubber stamping, caning, mosaic and other techniques, you can create a wide array of fun and functional polymer clay projects that will accent your home!

Baby
switchplate

decorative switchplates have become a popular way to enhance the décor of any room. They take up little space but can be a stylish accent on any wall in your home. Yes, you can bake a plastic switchplate in the oven! Rubber-stamping and sculpting create the perfect accessory for any baby's room. What a great idea for a newborn gift! Your handiwork is sure to become a treasured memory-box keepsake!

materials

- polymer clay

    1 black block
    1 blue block
    1 hot pink block
    2 pearl blocks
    1 white block
    1 yellow block

- small (PC5H) heart pattern cutter

- baby-themed rubber stamp

- plastic switchplate

- superglue

- ball-tip stylus

- craft knife

- needle tool

- tweezers

- gloss-finish polymer clay glaze (optional)

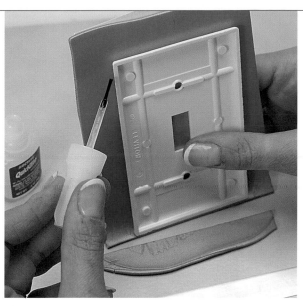

1 Mix and Stamp the Clay

Choose either baby blue or pastel pink for the base of the switchplate. To make baby blue clay, mix ¾ block of pearl clay with ⅛ block of blue clay. To make pastel pink clay, mix ¾ block of pearl clay with ⁄₁₆ block of hot pink clay. To make the pastel yellow you need for this project, mix ⅛ block of yellow with ⅛ block of white clay. Roll the clay for the base through the second-largest setting of the pasta machine. Impress the clay sheet with the rubber stamp.

2 Cover the Switchplate

Brush superglue over the plastic switchplate and apply the stamped clay. Apply additional glue along the edges and corners of the switchplate to secure the clay. Trim the excess clay from the edges with the clay blade.

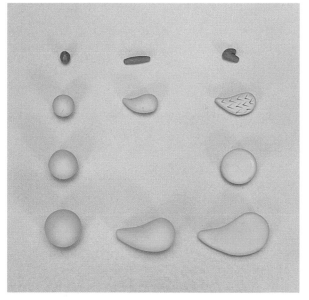

3 Trim the Clay From the Openings

Cut the clay from the switch opening with a craft knife. Use a needle tool to open the holes for the screws. Trim the clay away from the screw holes with the tip of the craft knife.

4 Create the Duck

To make the beak, roll a tiny pinch of orange clay into a small snake and bend it into a V shape. To make the wing, roll a ¼" (6mm) ball of pastel yellow clay into a teardrop shape, slightly flatten it with your fingertip, and bend the pointed end up. Make feather marks in the wing with the tip of your craft knife. For the duck's body, roll a ⁷⁄₁₆" (4mm) ball of pastel yellow clay into a teardrop shape. Bend the tip up to form a tail. Slightly flatten the body with your fingers.

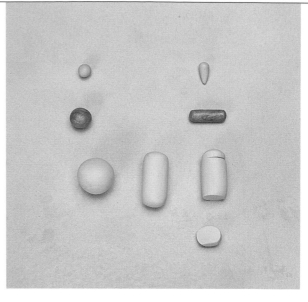

5 Glue the Duck to the Switchplate

Superglue the duck's body and head onto a corner of the switchplate. Apply the beak and wing with superglue as well. Add an eye by making a small hole on the head with a needle tool. Roll a tiny pinch of black clay into a ball and insert it into the hole.

6 Make the Bottle

To make the bottle, roll a small pinch of pastel yellow clay into a teardrop shape. For the bottle collar, roll a ¼" (6mm) ball of pastel pink or baby blue clay into a ⅜" (1cm) snake. To create the nipple, roll a ⁷⁄₁₆" (4mm) ball of white clay into a ⅝" (2cm) snake. Slightly flatten the white clay with your fingers.

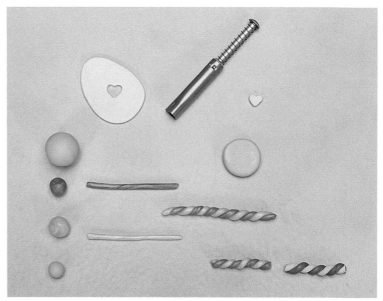

7 Glue the Bottle to the Switchplate

Superglue the bottle components to upper-right corner of the switchplate. Make vertical lines in the bottle collar with the edge of the craft knife.

8 Create the Rattle

Roll a small pinch of white clay through the fourth-largest setting of the pasta machine. Punch out a tiny heart with the pattern cutter. Roll a ⁷⁄₁₆" (4mm) ball of pastel yellow clay. Slightly flatten this ball with your fingers. To make the handle of the rattle, roll pinches of white and pastel pink clay (or white and baby blue clay for a pink switchplate) into two snakes ⅛" (3mm) in diameter. Twist the snakes together. Trim the twisted clay to ¾" (2cm) with the craft knife. For the end of the handle, roll a ⅜" (1cm) ball of pastel yellow clay. Slightly flatten the small yellow clay ball between your fingers.

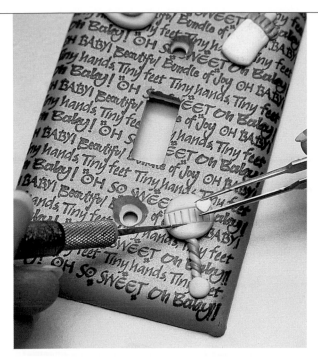

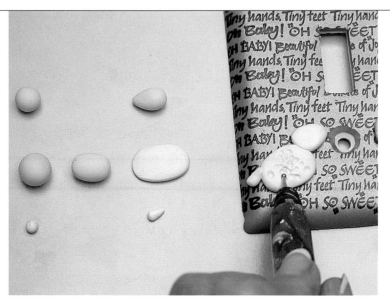

9 Glue the Rattle onto the Switchplate

Superglue the rattle components to the switchplate. Make decorative score marks in the rattle with the tip of the craft knife. Superglue the heart to the center of the rattle.

10 Add the Lamb

To create the head, roll a ³/₈" (1cm) ball of white clay into a stubby teardrop shape. For the body, roll a ¹/₁₆" (4mm) ball of white clay into an oval shape. Slightly flatten the oval with your fingers. To make the tail, roll a small pinch of white clay into a tiny teardrop shape. Superglue the lamb's body, head and tail to the switchplate. Stipple the lamb's body, tail and the back half of the head (leaving the nose smooth) with the small end of a ball-tip stylus.

11 Detail the Lamb

Roll five ³/₁₆" (5mm) balls of pastel pink (or baby blue for a pink switchplate) into teardrops. Press two of the teardrops together to make the front and back legs. Superglue the legs to the switchplate, under the lamb's body. Superglue the ear to the lamb's head. Slightly flatten the ear with your fingertip. To add the eye, make a small hole with tip of your needle tool. Roll a tiny pinch of black clay into a ball and insert it into the hole. For the nose, roll a slightly larger pinch of black clay into a ball and press it over the front of the lamb's face. Bake the switch plate at 270° F (132° C) for thirty minutes. Allow it to cool completely before hanging.

> **Dip the small end of a ball tip stylus** into polymer clay glaze-finish and touch it on the eyes, giving the lamb's and the duck's eyes a little extra sparkle.
>
> # TIP

Falling Leaves
candle holder

h ere are some leaves that won't need raking! Stamped and gilded leaves make this votive a cozy way to light up any autumn evening. A millefiori border finishes off this project. All you need to add is a candle and flame to add cheer to those blustery fall nights. Not in the mood for candlelight? This charming vessel makes a wonderful potpourri bowl, too!

materials

- polymer clay
  - 1 alizarin crimson block
  - 1 burnt umber block
  - 1 ecru block
  - 1 orange block
  - 1 raw sienna block
- gold pearlized powder

- large maple leaf rubber stamp
- glass rose bowl with 4" (10cm) diameter opening
- superglue
- small-gauge knitting needle
- eye shadow applicator (optional)

1 Stamp the Maple Leaves

Roll ½ block each of ecru, orange, raw sienna, burnt umber and alizarin crimson clays through the third-largest setting of the pasta machine. Spray the clay sheet with automotive protectant and make two to three impressions with the rubber stamp. Remember to work from lightest to darkest colors.

2 Cut Out the Leaf Shapes

When stamping, be sure to apply enough pressure to leave a detailed impression. Cut out the leaves with the craft knife.

3 Glue the Leaves to the Glass Bowl

Superglue the leaves randomly around the outside of the bowl. Be sure to place leaves over the upper and bottom edges of the bowl. Trim overhanging portions of leaves with the clay blade.

4 Highlight the Texture of the Leaves

Dip your fingertip or an eye shadow applicator into the gold pearlized powder. Lightly brush the powder over the surface of each leaf.

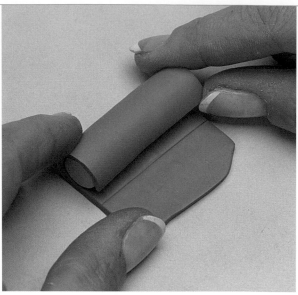

5 Begin Making the Bull's-Eye Cane

Roll ⅛ block of ecru clay into a 2" (5cm) snake. Cut off the distorted ends.

6 Add Orange Clay

Roll ½ block of orange clay through the second-largest setting of the pasta machine. Wrap the ecru snake with the orange clay sheet and trim the excess clay.

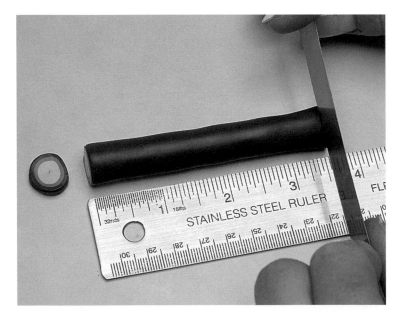

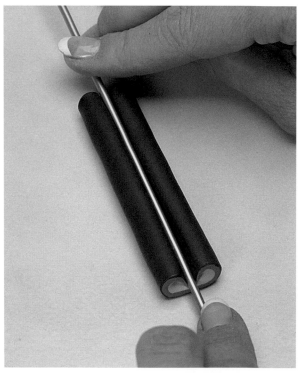

7 Add Burnt Umber Clay

Roll ½ block of burnt umber clay through the third-largest setting of the pasta machine. Wrap the ecru and orange cane with the burnt umber clay and trim the excess. Roll this cane back and forth over the work surface with your palm or fingers until the snake lengthens to 3" (8cm). Trim off the distorted ends.

8 Create Two Connecting Teardrops

Press a small-gauge knitting needle over the length of the trimmed cane. Push the knitting needle two-thirds of the way down through the center of the cane and remove.

9 Press the Cane Into One Teardrop

Pinch the separated cane halves together between your thumb and forefinger along the length to form a teardrop shape. Allow the cane to rest or freeze for fifteen minutes.

10 Slice the Teardrop Cane

Cut several dozen $\frac{1}{16}$" (1.5mm) thick slices from the cane. Flip the cane back and forth between each slice to prevent distorting the shape of the cane.

11 Add the Edging to the Bowl

Superglue the slices along the bowl's rim in a scallop fashion. Bake the candle holder at 270° F (132° C) for thirty minutes. Add a votive or pillar candle when cool.

Mosaic Address plaque

osaics never go out of style. This ancient art form has been around for thousands of years in cultures throughout the world. Cutting tiles from traditional materials like glass and ceramic can be difficult and time consuming. Why not make your own polymer clay mosaic tiles! The one-step, no-mess inlay technique used in this project makes mosaic-making a snap! Add a touch of ancient beauty to your home with this lovely address plaque. Once you learn how to make polymer clay mosaics, just think of all of the creative possibilities for future projects.

materials

- polymer clay
  - 1 blue block
  - 1 black block
  - 1 yellow block
  - 1 white block
- liquid polymer clay
- Phthalo Blue acrylic paint
- wood address plaque

- epoxy
- superglue
- tracing paper
- acrylic rod or brayer
- craft knife
- tweezers (optional)

2 Make Small Tiles

Roll out ¹⁄₂ block of blue clay on fourth-largest setting of the pasta machine. Lay the clay sheet on a smooth ceramic tile. Score the clay by pressing the clay blade into the clay every ¹⁄₄" (6mm). Turn the blade 90° to make score lines every ¹⁄₄" (6mm), creating squares. Repeat this step with ¹⁄₄ block of yellow clay. Make the white tiles ¹⁄₄" x ¹⁄₈" (6mm x 3mm). Bake the clay-covered ceramic tile at 270° F (132° C) for twenty minutes. Note: Getting perfectly even squares isn't necessary. Varying the sizes and shapes of the tiles indicates that the mosaic is handmade and lends to its charm. Some of these tiles will also need additional cutting to fit into oddly shaped areas.

1 Paint the Edges of the Plaque

Using two coats of the blue acrylic paint, paint the edges of the wooden address plaque and set aside to dry. Neatness doesn't count here!

Air trapped in clay expands with the heat of the oven, forming air pockets. If you discover this has happened after baking, place the plaque in a 270° F (132° C) oven for ten to fifteen minutes. Remove the plaque and poke a few holes between the tiles and grout with the tip of a craft knife. Set a telephone book over the plaque and weigh it down with several more heavy books. Allow the plaque to cool slowly under the weight of the books. This should remove any trapped air. **TIP**

3 Create the Grout

While the tile sheets are baking, roll out two combined blocks of black clay on the largest setting of the pasta machine. Cut this sheet in a rectangle, approximately 4" x 10" (10cm x 25cm) or slightly larger than the plaque surface. Mix a generous amount of two-part epoxy and spread the glue over the face of the plaque. Place the black clay sheet over the glued surface. Smooth this clay from the center of the plaque, working out any air that may be trapped underneath while the glue is setting.

4 Create and Transfer Your Template

Use a ruler to draw a 10" (25cm) line across a sheet of tracing paper. Mark the center point with another line perpedicular to the first. Use these lines as guide for placing your address number evenly on the tracing paper. Numerals should be 2" (5cm) tall, and may be hand-drawn or printed from a computer and drawn onto tracing paper. Center the tracing paper over black clay and cut through the numbers with a craft knife. Then remove the tracing paper.

5 Break Apart the Clay Tiles

After the clay sheets have baked and cooled, slide a clay blade under them to lift them off of the ceramic tile. Break the tiles apart at the score lines.

6 Use the Right Side of the Tiles

The underside of tiles bakes on ceramic will have a mottled, shiny appearance (shown above, at right) that may not be noticeable under certain lighting conditions. Be sure to keep the matte side (above, left) up while laying your tiles so the surface of your plaque will have a consistent finish.

7 Lay the Tiles

Using tweezers, lay the yellow tiles into the marked number areas. Use the craft knife to cut the tiles as needed for corners and smaller areas. Once the yellow tiles are laid, press them into the grout with your fingertips.

8 Fill In With Blue Tiles and Add the White Border

Following the outline of the yellow tiles as closely as possible, fill in the area between the numbers with blue tiles, pressing them into the grout as you go. Once the area between the numbers is filled, continue laying blue tiles around the numbers until two or three outer rows are laid. Leave at least $1/4$" (6mm) of grout on the outer edge of the plaque's face for the white tile border. Follow the outline of the blue tiles as closely as possible.

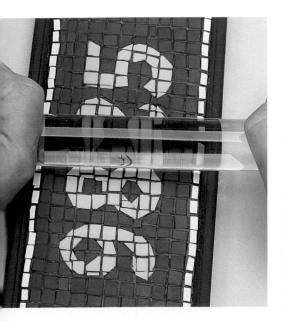

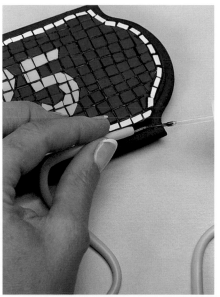

9 Embed the Tiles Into the Plaque

To ensure that all the tiles are properly seated in the grout, roll an acrylic rod or brayer over the surface of the plaque several times. It's not crucial that the surface be entirely level. Trim the excess grout from the upper edge of the plaque with the tip of the craft knife.

10 Add the Yellow Border

Roll $1/2$ block of yellow clay to a 26" (66cm) snake $3/16$" (5mm) in diameter. Superglue the snake around the outer edge of the mosaic surface. Cut off the excess clay and blend the seam together with your fingertip.

11 Add Final Touches

Add another $3/16$" (5mm) diameter snake of blue clay, measuring 28" (71cm) long, next to the yellow border. Bake the plaque at 270° F (132° C) for forty minutes.

polymer clay and garden décor

Few things are as gratifying and rewarding as planting something and watching it grow.

The popularity of gardening has risen dramatically in the last decade. This upsurge in interest is not necessarily due to need, but rather to the discovery of what so many gardeners already know: Gardening, and gardens themselves, can offer the serenity we so often seek from the hectic pace of our busy lives. These projects were created as a way to enhance any garden or bring a bit of nature indoors.

Garden stakes

this project is inspired by the time-honored tradition of identifying garden plants with seed packages. Copper tubing provides a durable and stylish support for these garden accessories, which are reminiscent of a simpler, less hurried time. Multitudes of people are rediscovering the joy of gardening. Whether you already have a green thumb or are just now discovering the delights of the garden, you'll be proud to show off these charming garden plaques.

materials

- polymer clay
  - 1 black block
  - 2 green blocks
  - 2 orange blocks
  - 2 red blocks
  - 3 white blocks
  - 1 yellow block
- small (PC2SQ) square pattern cutter
- small (PC1S) star pattern cutter
- small (PC2T) teardrop pattern cutter
- clay gun

- 3 pieces of ³⁄₈" (1cm) diameter copper tubing cut to 24" (61cm)
- 3 pieces of ³⁄₈" (1cm) diameter copper tubing cut to 6" (15cm)
- epoxy
- quilt batting
- superglue
- clay shaper
- craft knife
- needle tool

1 Begin the Carrot Stake

Roll one block of white clay through the largest setting of the pasta machine. Cut the clay into a 3¼" x 4¼" (8cm x 11cm) rectangle. Roll ⅛ block of orange clay through the fifth largest setting of the pasta machine. Cut out several dozen small clay squares with the small square pattern cutter. Place these around the outside edge of the clay, forming two checkerboard rows.

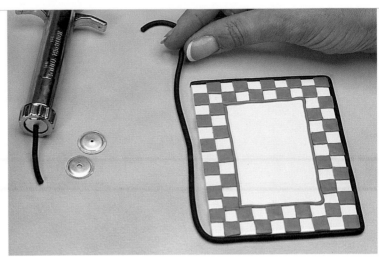

2 Create the Borders

Roll a ½" (1cm) ball of orange clay into a snake. Condition the clay very well, then load it into the clay gun. Press the gun's plunger to extrude an 11" (28cm) snake. Wrap the orange snake around the inside edge of checker-board border. Trim any excess clay. Load ⅛ block of well-conditioned black clay into a clean clay gun (see cleaning tip on page 13). Extrude a 16" (41cm) snake of clay. Superglue the black snake around the outside edges of the white clay.

> **TIP**
> If you don't have a clay gun, you may roll the border snakes by hand.

3 Make the Carrots

Roll one ¾" (2cm) and two ½" (1cm) balls of orange clay into crooked teardrop shapes. Slightly flatten the teardrops with your fingers to form three carrots. Place the large carrot in the center of the white clay. Mark horizontal lines along the entire length of the carrot with the tip of a craft knife to add texture. Place the two smaller carrots on either side of the large carrot, with bottom tips angling out. Texture the two small carrots with the craft knife.

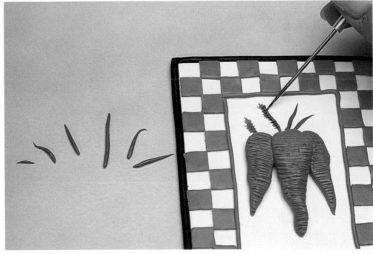

4 Add the Carrot Greens

Roll ten small pinches of green clay into very thin snakes. Cut these snakes about ¼"–½" (6mm–1cm) long, and place them at the tops of the carrots, fanning them out. Drag the green clay onto the white clay with the tip of the needle tool to create the feathery-looking leaves. Bake the panel at 270° F (132° C) for twenty-five minutes. Let cool.

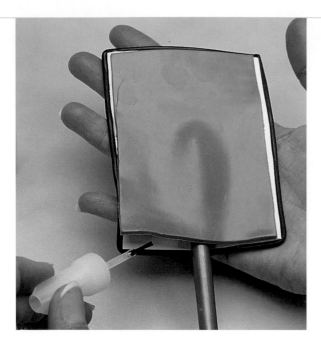

5 Add the Stake Backing

When the stake is cool, lay it face-down on a tile with a piece of quilt batting sandwiched in between (this supports the uneven surface of the clay). Roll out one block of orange clay on the largest setting of the pasta machine. Cut a 3" x 4" (8cm x 10cm) rectangle from the orange clay sheet. Lay a 6" (15cm) piece of copper tubing halfway up the back of the baked clay. Attach the backing with superglue, but do not brush glue too close to the copper tubing. Press out air pockets with your fingers.

6 Reinforce the Copper Tubing

Roll a 1/2" (1cm) ball of orange clay. Slightly flatten the ball between your fingers. Press it over the spot where the copper tubing sits under the orange clay. Blend the edges of the orange ball into the clay backing with a finger or clay shaper. Bake the stake on the batting and tile at 270° F (132° C) for forty minutes. When the stake is cool, twist the 6" (15cm) copper tube to loosen and remove it. Mix epoxy and insert it into the opening left from the tubing. Insert the 24" (61cm) copper tube into the glued opening. Let the glue set overnight before placing the stake in your garden.

7 Make the Tomatoes

Repeat steps 1 and 2 using black, white and red clay. Roll three 1/2" (1cm) balls of red clay into ovals. Slightly flatten and shape them into tomatoes with your fingers. Make three or four vertical lines down each tomato with a needle tool to add dimension.

8 Add the Tomato Greens

Roll a pinch of green clay through the fifth-largest setting of the pasta machine. Punch out three stars with the small star pattern cutter. Cut one arm off each star. Place a star over the top of each tomato. Shape the greens with your fingers. Place the tomatoes onto the center of the checkered clay.

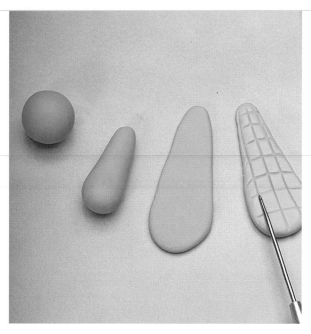

9 Add Leaves and Vines

Roll several small balls of green clay into thin snakes. Wind the snakes from the tomatoes around the face of the stake to create vines. Roll a large ball of green clay out on the fourth-largest setting of pasta machine. Cut out ten to twelve leaves with the teardrop pattern cutter. Make vein marks in the leaves with the tip of the needle tool. Place the leaves randomly along the vines. Finish the stake following steps 5 and 6 using red clay.

10 Begin the Corn Stake

Follow steps 1 and 2 using white, yellow and black clay. Roll a ¾" (2cm) ball of yellow clay into a 3" (8cm) long rounded-end teardrop. Flatten the teardrop against the work surface. Score intersecting lines into the clay with the tip of a craft knife to make corn kernels. Place the corn cob on the white clay at a slight angle (pointed end up).

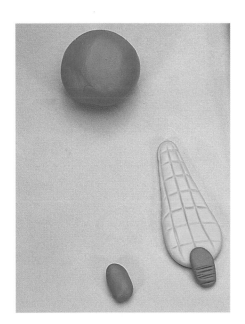

11 Create the Corn Stem

Mix ¼ block of green clay, 1/16 block of yellow clay, and 1/16 block of white clay together to make a light green clay. Roll a large pinch of light green into a short snake and flatten. Press this piece at the base of the corn cob for the stem.

12 Add the Husk

Roll the remaining light green clay through the fifth-largest setting of the pasta machine. Cut this sheet into five or six teardrop shapes of various sizes. Bend and fold creases into the teardrops with your fingers. Place the leaves around both sides of the corn cob, shaping as you go. Bake and finish following steps 5 and 6 using green clay.

Fantastic
flower pot

K eep the garden going all year long with this attractive planter. This flower pot is so colorful, it doesn't even need the plants! Millefiori flower petals, sculpted leaves and paint embellish an ordinary terra-cotta planter that will grace any windowsill. For those who lack a green thumb, this planter can be used as a charming holder for utensils, guest soaps or paintbrushes.

materials

- polymer clay

    1 black block
    1 fluorescent green block
    1 fuchsia block
    1 green block
    1 green pearl block
    1 pearl block
    1 purple block
    1 white block

- black gloss acrylic paint

- 3" (8cm) terra-cotta pot and saucer

- shingle-pattern rubbing plate (I used Shade-Tex Rubbing Plate)

- superglue

- needle tool

2 Add Light Green Pearl Clay

Mix one block of pearl clay and ¼ block of green pearl clay together to make a light green pearl clay. Roll out the light green pearl clay on the third-largest setting of the pasta machine. Trim a straight edge along one end and side of the pot. Align one straight edge of clay sheet under the pot rim and one along the glued line. Wrap the clay around the pot, gluing small sections as you wrap.

1 Prepare the Terra-Cotta Pot and Saucer

Prepare the pot by drawing eight evenly spaced marks on the bottom of the pot. Paint the saucer and upper rim of the pot with two coats of black gloss acrylic paint, then let dry.

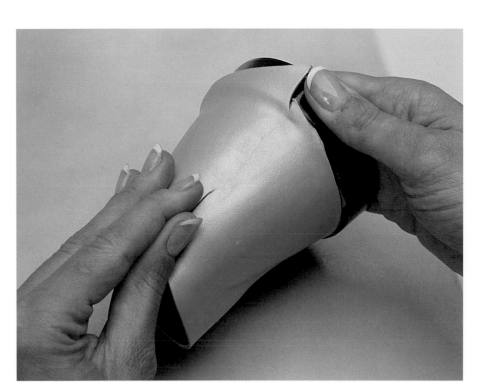

3 Blend the Seam

Once you have glued the clay to the pot, trim excess overlapping clay and blend the seam together with your fingertips or a clay shaper until you have a smooth, flat surface.

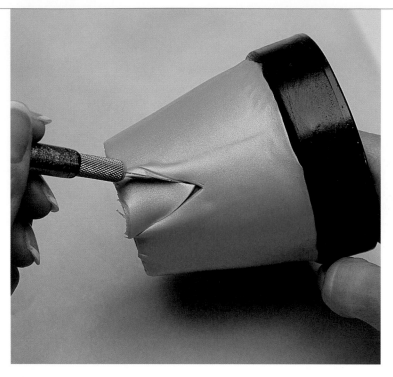

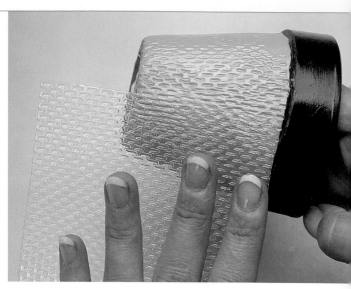

5 Add Texture to the Light Green Pearl Clay

Cut a square from the shingle-pattern rubbing plate, and press it into the surface of the trimmed green clay. Continue until the entire clay-covered area is textured.

4 Work Out Any Air Bubbles

Remove any air pockets that may have formed with your fingers and trim the overlapping clay. Cut the excess clay from around the rim and bottom of the pot.

6 Create the Flower Stems

Roll ⅛ block of green and fluorescent green clay into 3" (8cm) snakes. Run each snake through the largest setting of the pasta machine. Roll ¹⁄₁₆ block of white clay into a 3" (8cm) snake and run it through the fifth-largest setting of the pasta machine. Sandwich the white clay sheet between the two green sheets. Trim the stacked clay sheets into a rectangle with a clay blade. Cut eight ¹⁄₁₆" (2mm) thick strips from this stacked clay block and twist. Superglue the twists onto the pot using the bottom pencil markings as a placement guide. Cut away the excess clay. Press the indented areas of each twist with a needle tool to secure the clay to the pot.

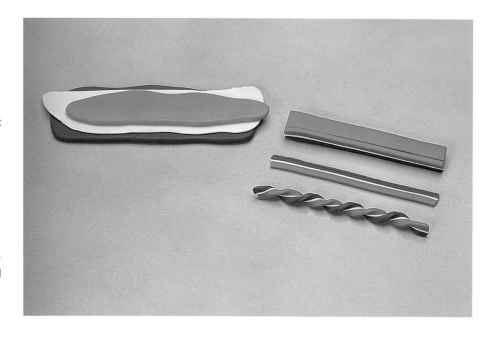

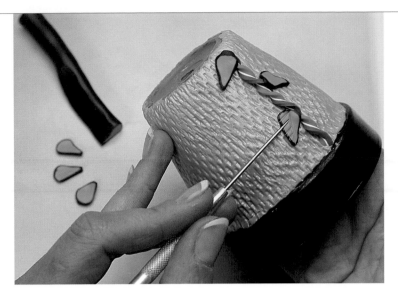

7 Make the Leaves

Roll ¼ block of fluorescent green clay into a snake ⅝" (1cm) in diameter. Roll ¼ block of black clay through the fourth-largest setting of the pasta machine and wrap it around the green snake. Trim away the excess clay. Roll to reduce the wrapped snake to ½" (1cm) in diameter. Cut off the distorted ends. Pinch the wrapped snake along its length, between your thumb and index finger into a teardrop shape. Let the cane rest or freeze for fifteen minutes. Slice about twenty ⅛" (3mm) thick slices from cane. Superglue two to three of these leaf slices along each of the eight stems. Mark vein lines into the leaves with the tip of the needle tool.

8 Add Leaves to the Saucer

Slice about twenty-two ⅛" (3mm) slices from the cane. Super-glue the leaf slices around the entire edge of the painted saucer in a scallop fashion.

9 Add the Flower Petals

Make a white and fuchsia Skinner Blend cane following the directions on pages 14–15. Wrap the cane with purple clay rolled through the second-largest setting. Then wrap again with white clay rolled through the fifth-largest setting. Wrap once again with black clay rolled through the fourth-largest setting on pasta machine. Roll and reduce this cane to ¾" (2cm) in diameter. Cut off a 1" (3cm) section from the cane and pinch it into a teardrop shape. Cut twenty-four ¹⁄₁₆" (2mm) thick slices. Cut a 1" (3cm) section from the remaining cane and reduce it to ⅜" (1cm) in diameter. Pinch the cane into a teardrop and cut eight slices. Each flower requires three large petals and one small petal in front. Superglue the petals to the pot and bake the pot and saucer at 270° F (132° C) for thirty-five minutes.

Garden
angel

angels aren't just for people. Let this graceful cherub nurture the life in your garden as she sits protectively among the flowers. Simple sculpting techniques will allow you to make the angel and the roses that adorn her flowing gown. Learn how to make beautiful wings with a leather embossing techniques and pattern cutters. Simple, but suggestive of divine grace, this angel will add a touch of charm and serenity to any garden.

materials

- polymer clay

  - 1 beige block
  - 1 green pearl block
  - 1 gold block
  - 1 fuchsia block
  - 2 pearl blocks
  - 1 purple block
  - 1 violet block
  - 1 white block
  - 1" (3cm) ball of scrap clay

- leaf leather-working stamp

- small (PC5F), medium (PC3F) and large (PC2F) flower pattern cutters

- small (PC2T) teardrop pattern cutter

- 2½" (6cm) heart cookie cutter

- 1 piece of ⅜" (1cm) diameter copper tubing cut to 4" (10cm)

- 1 piece of ⅜" (1cm) diameter copper tubing cut to 24" (61cm)

- aluminum foil

- automotive protectant

- epoxy

- superglue

- ball-tip stylus

- toothpicks

1 Make a Stand for the Angel

Slightly flatten a 1" (3cm) clay ball against your work surface with the palm of your hand. Insert the 4" (10cm) piece of copper tubing into the center of this ball to make a baking stand. Bake the stand at 270° F (132° C) for forty minutes. Allow it to cool. Crumple a 24"(61cm) sheet of aluminum foil into a loose ball. Press the foil ball onto the copper tubing of the cooled stand. Shape and tightly compress the foil into a football shape.

2 Create the Angel's Skirt

Roll a block of pearl clay through the largest setting of the pasta machine. Cut out a large oval from this sheet. Mix a small amount of epoxy and spread it over the top of the foil. Drape the clay oval over the glued foil to form a skirt.

3 Add the Torso

Shape the skirt with your fingers, forming pleats in the sides and back. Roll the clay remaining from the oval into a short, stubby teardrop shape for the torso. Insert a toothpick halfway through the top of the skirt and connect the torso to the skirt.

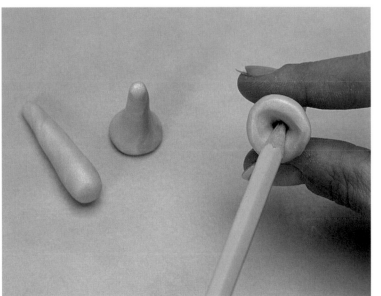

4 Make the Angel's Arms

Roll two $^{1}/_{16}$ blocks of pearl clay into teardrops. Flatten the large ends of each teardrop by pressing them against the work surface. Insert a sharpened pencil into the flattened ends and rotate, flaring out the sleeves.

5 Add the Hands

Roll two ½" (1cm) balls of beige clay into teardrops. Slightly flatten the large end of each teardrop between your thumb and index finger. Brush superglue onto the pointed ends of each teardrop and insert them into the ends of the sleeves. Bend the hands inward toward the center of the body.

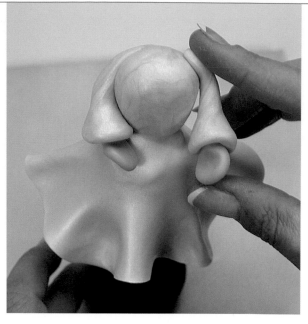

6 Attach the Arms to the Torso

Press the narrow end of each arm onto the shoulder area of the angel's torso. Smooth the clay where the shoulder meets the torso to secure.

7 Make the Rosebuds

Roll twenty ¼" (6mm) balls of fuchsia clay into ⅞" (2cm) long snakes. Flatten these snakes between your fingers. Begin at one end of each flattened snake and roll inward until you reach the end. Continue rolling snakes to form rosebuds.

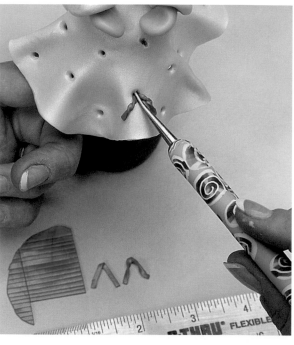

8 Create the Setting for the Rosebuds

Randomly poke twenty holes around the skirt with the needle tool. Run ¹⁄₁₆ block of green pearl clay through the fifth-largest setting of the pasta machine. Cut twenty ¾" x ¹⁄₁₆" (1cm x 2mm) strips from the green pearl clay. Lift each strip with the point of the needle tool and place one at the bottom of each hole in the skirt. Twist the ends of the green clay strips one or two times.

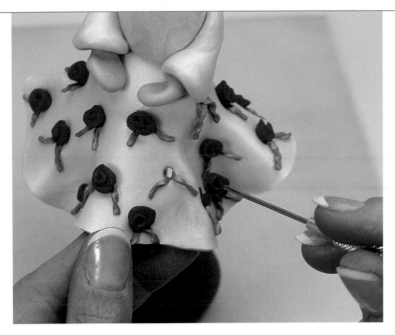

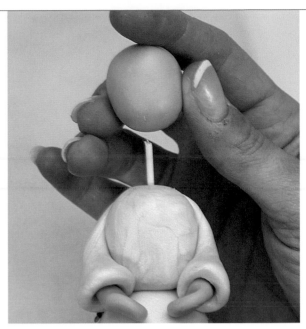

9 Secure the Rosebuds in Place

Place a dot of superglue in the holes of the skirt (gluing only three or four holes at a time). Insert the pointed ends of the rosebuds into the glued holes with the needle tool. Repeat until all the roses are inserted into the holes.

10 Add the Angel's Head

Insert a toothpick halfway into the top of the angel's torso. Roll a ¾" (2cm) ball of beige clay and add the angel's head.

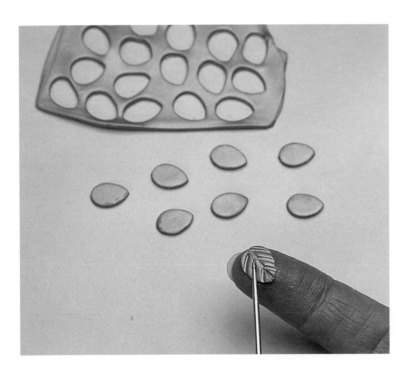

11 Make Golden Leaves for the Hair

Roll ⅛ block of gold clay through the fourth-largest setting of the pasta machine. Punch out several dozen leaf shapes with the teardrop pattern cutter. Make vein lines in the leaves with the tip of the needle tool.

12 Add the Hair

Starting from the shoulders, scallop the leaves, one over the other, up and over the head to make "leaf hair."

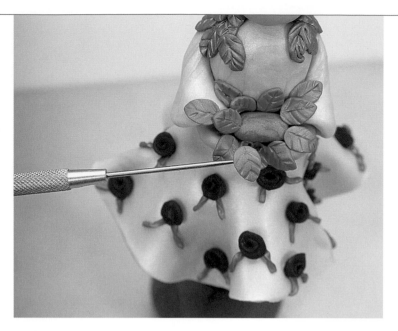

13 Add the Bouquet Leaves

Roll a ⅜" (1cm) ball of green pearl clay into an oval and press it into the angel's hands. Run ⅛ block of green pearl clay through the fourth-largest setting of the pasta machine. Punch out twelve leaf shapes and make veins as in step 11. Press the leaves around the clay oval, spilling onto the arms, torso and hands of the angel.

14 Create the Flowers

Roll purple and fuchsia clay through the fourth-largest setting of the pasta machine. Cut out several dozen flowers using all three sizes of the flower pattern cutters. Place the smallest flowers randomly over the angel's head and shoulders. Insert the tip of the stylus into the center of each flower, securing them to the clay.

15 Detail the Flower Bouquet

Place the medium and large flowers over the leaves in the angel's hands. Insert tiny balls of gold and white clay into the flower centers. Stipple the centers with the tip of the needle tool.

16 Begin to Make the Halo

Chop pinches of white, fuchsia and purple clay into tiny pieces with a clay blade.

17 Form the Halo

Using the needle tool, place bits of the chopped clay around the angel's head to form a flower petal halo.

18 Begin to Make the Wings

Roll ½ block of green pearl clay through the fourth-largest setting of the pasta machine. Spray the clay sheet with automotive protectant and spread it with your fingers. Impress the entire clay sheet with the leaf leather-working stamp. Cut out two clay hearts from the stamped clay with the cookie cutter to form the wings.

19 Create the Wing Border

Superglue the hearts together, stamped sides facing out. Roll ⅛ block of green pearl clay through the fourth-largest setting of the pasta machine. Punch out twenty-four leaves with the small teardrop pattern cutter and make vein lines in each leaf. Starting from the bottom of the wings, superglue and wrap each leaf along the wings' edge, scalloping one leaf over the other until both sides of the heart are covered. Finish off the wings by adding a leaf at the top and bottom points of the heart.

20 Attach the Wings to the Angel

Brush superglue on the lower portion of the angel's back and the back of the head. Carefully press the wings on the angel's back, making sure full contact is made between both pieces. Bake the angel on the stand at 270° F (132° C) for forty minutes. After the angel is cool, remove the 4" (10cm) copper tube and mix and insert the two-part epoxy into the hole of the foil. Reinsert the 24" (61cm) copper tube. Let the glue set for twenty-four hours before placing the angel in your garden. Store indoors during harsh winter months.

gallery

This section showcases a handful of artwork made by talented polymer clay artists, in addition to some pieces from my own collection. The diversity of these projects offers just a small sample of how versatile and inspiring this medium can be. The possibilities are as endless as your imagination!

▲ Business Card Holder Couch

This tiny, overstuffed sofa serves as a business card holder. The pillows prevent the cards from sliding off the cushions. Millefiori sheets were layered over aluminum and scrap clay armatures to create this piece.

▼ Teaspoon Cup

This whimsical teacup was made by layering millefiori swirls onto carved, frosted glass. Real teaspoons with millefiori embellishments were attached and serve as the cup's handle and feet.

▲ Purses

These minaudiére evening bags were created using metal and chipboard purse frames. A variety of techniques, including sculpting, millefiori, mokumé gané and mica shifting were used to create unique yet functional purses.

◄ Asian Vessel

A recycled hair-care product bottle is the base of this antique-looking vessel. Gold clay was impressed Japanese stamps for *health*, *happiness* and *long life*. It was baked and antiqued with burnt umber acrylic paint. The faux onyx, jade and cinnabar lid and embellishments were all made using polymer clay techniques.

◀ Faux Dichroic Plate

This platter was made by layering fabric foil-covered clay underneath a glass plate. Millefiori leaves adorn the edges of the platter and secure the clay to the glass. Small balls of violet clay placed between each leaf add visual interest to the entire plate.

▼ Berry Teapot

This usable teapot was made over a ceramic armature. The teapot is adorned with strawberries, raspberries, blackberries and blueberries. Each leaf and berry are individually hand-sculpted. Millefiori leaves accent the teapot lid.

▲ Daisy Bracelet

A flower garden was the inspiration for this delightful bracelet, designed and created by Sally Seiller. Most of the petals were made with mille-fiori canes to create a realistic look. The piece was finished with a metallic gold acrylic wash to enhance the depth and tone of the piece.

▶ Dragonfly Pins

These gorgeous dragonfly pins, created by Deborah Anderson, are made from millefiori cane slices. The wings have a thin layer of tinted translucent polymer clay placed over the cane work. A piece of wire goes through the body for added strength.

◄ Mosaic Table

The top of this accent table was made with over three thousand hand-cut polymer clay tiles. The pattern was embedded in a layer of polymer clay grout, set over a ceramic tile, which was cut to fit into the wrought iron table base.

▼ Flower Pen & Stand

This refillable pen was created using a floral-pattern millefiori design. The pen was polished after baking. The stand was made over an foil armature and covered with hand-sculpted clay flowers.

▲ Faux Quilt Box

This elegant box was made by Irene Yurkewych using a mica shift parquetry technique and just one shade of metallic clay. Light refraction off the mica particles creates the illusion of varied coloration and texture. This technique requires patience and precision, but the results are well worth the effort.

► Enchanting Vessels

These vessels were made by wrapping a Skinner Blended clay sheet over a light bulb (a technique developed by Jody Bishell). The light bulb was broken and removed after baking. Exterior embellishments, lids, and feet were added before additional bakings.

◀ Autumn Necklace

This striking neckpiece was created by Jill Akiron-Moses using many variations on the Skinner blend. Rich autumnal colors of ochre, gold, copper and russet are further enhanced by the addition of leaves created from translucent clay and gold leaf. Vibrantly patterned spacer beads enhance the overall visual interest of the piece.

▲ Exotic Sculptured Vessels

Laura Timmons created these splendid sculptural vessels by sandwiching polymer clay over a wire mesh armature. The layered sheets of clay are embellished with cane work and then joined, stretched and bent by hand into its final form. Delicately twisted ropes of clay adorn the edge of the vessel.

◀ Mardi Gras Mask

Anne Igou created this magnificent, wearable Mardi Gras Mask. It is made from stamped polymer clay leaves and embellished with flecks of gold leaf and iridescent powders.

AARON BROTHERS ▸ 1270 S. Goodrich Blvd., Commerce, CA 90022; Telephone: (888) 532-9372; Fax: (323) 888-4600; www.aaronbros.com ▸ *photo storage boxes*

ACCENT IMPORT-EXPORT, INC. ▸ 1501 Loveridge Rd., Box 18, Pittsburg, CA 94565; Telephone: (800) 989-2889; Fax: (925) 431-1152; www.fimozone.com ▸ *polymer clays, tools and accessories*

ALL NIGHT MEDIA ▸ 4219 Ashmont Ct., Dallas, TX 75287; Telephone: (972) 380-2596; Fax: (972) 355-6395; www.allnightmedia.com ▸ *Leaf stamp #846J*

AMERICAN ART CLAY CO., INC. (AMACO) ▸ 4717 W. 16th St., Indianapolis, IN 46222-2598; Telephone: (800) 374-1600; Fax: (317) 248-9300; www.amaco.com ▸ *polymer clay, gold leaf, craft wire, wire mesh embossing metal, millefiori canes, molds and tools*

APPLIANCES.COM ▸ 11558 SR 44, Mantua, OH 44255; Telephone: (888) 543-8345; Fax: (330) 274-2031; www.appliances.com ▸ *pasta machines and motors*

ARTISTIC WIRE ▸ 1210 Harrison Ave., LaGrange Park, IL 60526; Telephone: (630) 530-7567; Fax: (630) 530-7536; www.artisticwire.com ▸ *craft wire*

ATECO (AUGUST THOMSEN CORP.) ▸ 36 Sea Cliff Ave., Glen Cove, NY 11542; Telephone: (800) 645-7170; Fax: (516) 676-7180 ▸ *circle and heart cookie cutters*

BEADS PLUS ▸ 4750 W. Sahara Ave., Ste. 13, Las Vegas, NV 89102; Telephone: (702) 259-6100; Fax: (702) 259-6900; www.beadsplus.com ▸ *flat-backed crystals, glass beads and findings*

BOOKS BY HAND ▸ 505 Cagua Dr. S.E., Albuquerque, NM 87108; Telephone: (505) 255-3534; Fax: (505) 255-3634; bookbinder@aol.com ▸ *decorative papers, including gold scallop paper*

THE CLAY FACTORY OF ESCONDIDO ▸ 54310 Pleasant Valley Dr., Osceola, IN 46561; Telephone: (800) 622-5131; Fax: (219) 674-0649; www.clayfactory.com ▸ *polymer clays, tools, accessories, books and videos*

CLEARSNAP ▸ P.O. Box 98, Anacortes, WA 98221; Telephone: (800) 448-4862; Fax: (360) 293-6699; www.clearsnap.com ▸ *rubber stamp pads*

CRAF-T-PEDLARS ▸ 1009-D Shary Cir., Concord, CA 94518; Telephone: (877) PEDLARS; Fax: (877) 4PEDLARS; www.craftpedlars.com ▸ *Papier-mâché boxes*

DECOART ▸ P.O. Box 386, Stanford, KY 40484; Telephone: (800) 367-3043; Fax: (606) 365-9739; www.decoart.com ▸ *ultra-gloss and acrylic paints*

DELTA TECHNICAL COATINGS ▸ 2550 Pellisseir Pl., Whittier, CA 90601; Telephone: (800) 423-4135; Fax: (562) 695-4227; www.deltacrafts.com ▸ *acrylic paints*

DOVER PUBLICATIONS ▸ 31 E. 2nd St., Mineola, NY 11501-3852; Telephone: (516) 294-7000; Fax: (516) 742-6953; www.doverpublications.com ▸ *copyright-free clip art*

EMBOSSING ARTS ▸ P.O. Box 439, Tangent, OR 97389; Telephone: (800) 662-7955; www.embossingarts.com ▸ *clear checkbook holders*

FISKARS ▸ 7811 W. Stewart Ave., Wausau, WI 54401; Telephone: (800) 950-0203; Fax: (715) 928-9898; www.fiskars.com ▸ *decorative edging scissors and rotary cutters*

HAMPTON ART STAMPS ▸ 19 Industrial Blvd., Medford, NY 11763; Telephone: (631) 924-1335; Fax: (631) 924-1669; www.uimprint.com ▸ *rubber stamps*

HEART IN HAND STUDIO ▸ 9825 Tarzana Lane, Las Vegas, NV 89117; Telephone: (702) 243-6564; www.heartinhandstudio.com ▸ *business card blanks*

HIROMI PAPER INTERNATIONAL ▸ 2525 Michigan Ave., #G-9, Santa Monica, CA 90404; Telephone: (310) 998-0098; Fax: (310) 998-0028; www.hiromipaper.com ▸ *decorative papers, including gold crinkle paper*

INKADINKADO ▸ 61 Holton St., Woburn, MA 01801; Telephone: (781) 938-6100; Fax: (781) 938-5585; www.inkadinkado.com ▸ *baby rubber stamp #6697-Q*

JONES TONES ▸ 33865 United Ave., Pueblo, CO 81001; Telephone: (719) 948-0048; Fax: (719) 948-3348; www.jonestones.com ▸ *fabric foils*

JUDIKINS ▸ 17803 S. Harvard Blvd., Gardena, CA 90248; Telephone: (310) 515-1115 ; Fax: (310) 515-1115; www.judikins.com ▸ *rubber stamps*

THE LEATHER FACTORY ▸ 3847 E. Loop 820 S., Ft. Worth, TX 76119; Telephone: (800) 433-3201 ; Fax: (817) 492-9255; www.leatherfactory.com ▸ *leather stamping tools*

KEMPER ENTERPRISES ▸ 31595 12th Street, Chino, CA 91710; Telephone: (800) 388-5367; Fax: (909) 627-4008 ▸ *Kemper pattern cutters, ball-tip stylus, clay blades, tools*

THE MAGNET SOURCE ▸ 607 Gilbert, Castle Rock, CO 80104; Telephone: (888) 298-3534; Fax: (303) 688-5303; www.magnetsource.com ▸ *adhesive-backed magnet sheets*

MANCO INC. ▸ 32150 Just Imagine Dr., Avon, OH 44011-1355; Telephone: (800) 321-0253; Fax: (440) 937-7077; Website: www.manco.com ▸ *Brush-on superglue, two-part epoxy, double-sided adhesive and acrylic spray sealers*

PERSONAL STAMP EXCHANGE ▸ 360 Sutton Pl., Santa Rosa, CA 95407; Telephone: (800) 782-6748 ; Fax: (707) 588-7476; www.psxdesign.com ▸ *rubber stamps*

POLYFORM PRODUCTS ▸ 1901 Estes Ave., Elk Grove Village, IL 60007; Telephone: (847) 427-0020; Fax: (847) 427-0426; www.sculpey.com ▸ *Premo Sculpey, Sculpey III, Liquid Sculpey, clay blades, molds and tools*

POLYMER CLAY EXPRESS ▸ 13017 Wisteria Dr., Box 275, Germantown, MD 20874; Telephone: (800) 844-0138; Fax: (301) 482-0610; www.polymerclayexpress.com ▸ *polymer clay, tools, accessories, books and videos*

PRAIRIE CRAFT COMPANY ▸ P.O. Box 209, Florissant, CO 80816-0209; Telephone: (800) 779-0615; Fax: (719) 748-5112; www.prairiecraft.com ▸ *polymer clay, tools, accessories, books and videos*

RIO GRANDE ▸ 7500 Bluewater Rd. NW, Albuquerque, NM 87121-1962; Telephone: (800) 545-6566; Fax: (800) 965-2329; www.riogrande.com ▸ *silver charms, crystals, jewelry findings and accessories*

RUPERT, GIBBON & SPIDER INC. (JACQUARD) ▸ P.O. Box 425, Healdsburg, CA 95448; Telephone: (800) 442-0455; Fax: (707) 433-4906; www.jacquardproducts.com ▸ *pearl powders*

SANFORD ▸ 2711 Washington Blvd., Bellwood, IL 60104; Telephone: (800) 323-0749; Fax: (708) 547-6719; www.sanfordcorp.com ▸ *colored pencils and permanent markers*

SCRATCH ART CO., INC. ▸ P.O. Box 303, 11 Robbie Rd. Avon, MA 02322; Telephone: (502) 583-8085; Fax: (508) 583-8091; www.scratchart.com ▸ *texture plates*

STAMP OASIS ▸ 4750 W. Sahara Ave. Ste. 17 , Las Vegas, NV 89102; Telephone: (702) 878-6474; Fax: (702) 070 7021; www.stampoasis.com ▸ *Rubber stamps, Luna Lights pearl paint, pearl powders*

TONER PLASTICS ▸ 699 Silver St., Agawam, MA 01001; Telephone: (413) 789-1300; Fax: (413) 789-1144 ; www.tonerplastics.com ▸ *plastic-coated wire*

WALNUT HOLLOW ▸ 1409 SR 23, Dodgeville, WI 53533; Telephone: (800) 950-5101; Fax: (608) 935-3029; www.walnuthollow.com ▸ *wooden plaques*

WEE FOLK CREATIONS ▸ 18476 Natchez Avenue, Prior Lake, MN 55372; Telephone: (952) 447-3828; Fax: (952) 447-8816; www.weefolk.com ▸ *polymer clays, tools, accessories, books and videos*

WRIGHTS ▸ 85 South St., P.O. Box 398, W. Warren, MA 01092; Telephone: (877) 597-4448; Fax: (413) 436-9785; www.wrights.com ▸ *chenille lace-up cord*

Websites

POLYMER CLAY CENTRAL: www.polymerclaycentral.com ▸ *One of the oldest and most comprehensive polymer clay websites. Filled with project and product information. Great resource for polymer clay links.*

POLYFORM PRODUCTS: www.sculpey.com ▸ *Lots of useful information including projects for children and adults; featuring Sculpey clays.*

POLYMER CLAY HAVEN: www.polymerclayhaven.com ▸ *A site devoted to promoting information and discussion on all things polymer.*

Further Reading

The Art of Polymer Clay: Designs and Techniques for Making Jewelry, Pottery and Decorative Artwork, Donna Kato, 1997; New York: Watson-Guptill Crafts.

Creative Ways with Polymer Clay, Dotty McMillan, 2001, New York: Sterling Publishing.

Creating Life-Like Animals in Polymer Clay, Katherine Dewey, 2000; Cincinnati, Ohio: North Light Books.

Family and Friends in Polymer Clay, Maureen Carlson, 2000; Cincinnati, Ohio: North Light Books.

Foundations in Polymer Clay Design, Barbara A. McGuire, 1999; Krause Publications.

Making Animal Characters in Polymer Clay, Sherian Frey, 2000; Cincinnati, Ohio: North Light Books.

The New Clay Techniques and Approaches to Jewelry Making, Nan Roche, 1992; Rockville, Maryland: Flower Valley Press.

New Ways with Polymer Clay: The Next Generation of Projects and Techniques, Kris Richards, 1997; Iola, Wisconsin: Krause.

The Polymer Clay Techniques Book, Sue Heaser, 1999; Cincinnati, OH: North Light Books.

Organizations

NATIONAL POLYMER CLAY GUILD ▸ 1350 Beverly Road, Suite 115-345, McLean, VI 22101; Telephone: (202) 895-5212; Website: wwwnpcg.org ▸ *National organization dedicated to polymer clay education. Yearly membership includes quarterly newsletter. A terrific resource for information on regional clay guilds and events.*

SOCIETY OF CRAFT DESIGNERS ▸ Website: www.craft-designers.org ▸ *Organization supporting professional craft designers for the craft and hobby industries.*

Publications

BEAD & BUTTON ▸ Telephone: (800) 533-6644; Website: www.beadandbutton.com ▸ *Bimonthly magazine showcasing decorative wearables.*

CRAFTS REPORT ▸ Telephone: (888) 777-7098; Website: www.craftsreport.com ▸ *Monthly magazine devoted to the hobby-for-profit and professional crafter.*

JEWELRY CRAFTS ▸ Telephone: (800) 528-1024; Website: www.jewelrycrafts@pcspublink.com ▸ *Bimonthly magazine devoted to jewelry making. Many projects feature polymer clay.*

LAPIDARY JOURNAL ▸ Telephone: (800) 676-4336; Website: www.lapidaryjournal.com ▸ *Monthly jewelry and gem magazine.*

ORNAMENT MAGAZINE ▸ Telephone: (800) 888-8950; Website: www.ornamentmagazine.com ▸ *Quarterly magazine featuring wearable art.*

index

The best polymer clay projects come from
North Light Books!

Filled with fresh designs, simple techniques and gorgeous colors, this exciting book combines two fun, easy-to-master crafts in one. You'll find guidelines for stamping images on all your clay creations, including jewelry, home décor and more, along with advice for experimenting with color and finish. The wide variety of projects guarantees delightfully unique results.

ISBN 1-58180-155-6, paperback, 128 pages, #31904-K

Now you can use polymer clay to create elegant designs for your home! Nineteen step-by-step projects make getting started easy. You'll learn how to combine clay with fabric, silverware and other household items. These projects use metallic powders that simulate colored glass, antique bronze or gleaming silver. You'll also find instructions for color mixing, marbling and caning.

ISBN 1-58180-139-4, paperback, 128 pages, #31880-K

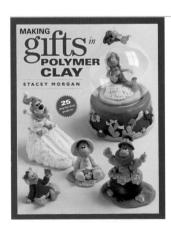

These twenty-one adorable projects perfectly capture the spirit of the seasons. Each one is wonderfully easy to make and can be completed in a single sitting. From leprechauns, Easter eggs, spooky witches and Thanksgiving turkeys to a polar bear on skis, there's something for everyone—including kids! You'll also find guidelines for creating magnets, buttons and pins.

ISBN 1-58180-104-1, paperback, 128 pages, #31792-K

Learn to sculpt delightful clay figures of your favorite people! This fun guide provides clear, step-by-step instructions that ensure immediate success. You'll also find a complete description of tools and supplies, general techniques for creating faces and bodies, plus tricks for recreating moods, expressions and features that capture the essence of a specific person.

ISBN 0-89134-927-8, paperback, 128 pages, #31542-K